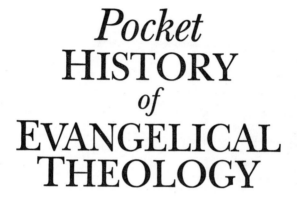

Pocket
HISTORY
of
EVANGELICAL
THEOLOGY

ROGER E. OLSON

InterVarsity Press
Downers Grove, Illinois

InterVarsity Press
P.O. Box 1400, Downers Grove, IL 60515-1426
World Wide Web: www.ivpress.com
E-mail: email@ivpress.com

InterVarsity Press® is the book-publishing division of InterVarsity Christian Fellowship/
USA®, a student movement active on campus at hundreds of universities, colleges and
schools of nursing in the United States of America, and a member movement of the
International Fellowship of Evangelical Students. For information about local and
regional activities, write Public Relations Dept., InterVarsity Christian Fellowship/USA,
6400 Schroeder Rd., P.O. Box 7895, Madison, WI 53707-7895, or visit the IVCF website
at <www.intervarsity.org>.

Design: Cindy Kiple
Images: Ronda Oliver/istockphoto.com

ISBN 978-0-8308-2706-0

Printed in the United States of America ∞

Library of Congress Cataloging-in-Publication Data

Olson, Roger E.
  Pocket history of evangelical theology / Roger E. Olson.
      p. cm.
  "Taken from the Westminster handbook to evangelical theology,
c2004"—T.p. verso. Includes bibliographical references. ISBN
978-0-8308-2706-0 (pbk.: alk. paper)
  1. Evangelicalism—History. 2. Theology, Doctrinal—History. I.
Olson, Roger E. Westminster handbook to evangelical theology. II.
Title.
  BR1640.O45 2007
  230'.0462409—dc22

                                                            2006101575

| P | 15 | 14 | 13 | 12 | 11 | 10 | 9 | 8 | 7 | 6 | 5 | 4 | 3 | 2 | 1 |
| Y | 19 | 18 | 17 | 16 | 15 | 14 | 13 | 12 | 11 | 10 | 09 | 08 | 07 |

Contents

1

Toward a Definition of Evangelicalism

Defining *evangelical, evangelicalism,* and *evangelical theology* has become something of a cottage industry in the waning years of the twentieth century and early years of the twenty-first century. At least since a national news magazine in the United States declared 1977 "The Year of the Evangelical," numerous religious scholars have attempted to provide a definitive portrait, if not concrete definition, of the term *evangelical* and the religious movement it describes. Entire scholarly conferences and symposia have devoted great effort and energy to the cause of investigating and finally comprehensively describing evangelicalism. Even some self-identified evangelical scholars have declared *evangelical* an essentially contested concept—an idea and category with no precise or agreed-on meaning.[1] In fact, so

[1]See Donald W. Dayton, "Some Doubts about the Usefulness of the Category 'Evangelical'" in *The Variety of American Evangelicalism,* ed. Donald W. Dayton and Robert K. Johnston (Downers Grove, IL: InterVarsity Press, 1991), 245-51.

it seems, there are several justifiable uses of the term *evangelical*. They are all legitimized by either broad historical usage or common contemporary usage. Here we will delineate seven distinct though occasionally overlapping meanings of *evangelical* and then identify which one of them is intended by the title of this handbook and will be its subject.

Etymologically *evangelical* simply means "of the good news" or "related to the gospel." The Greek root, a word for "good message" or "good news," was used by the apostles of Christianity and the early Greek-speaking church fathers for the gospel they proclaimed. In this broadest sense of *evangelical*, then, *evangelicalism* is simply synonymous with authentic Christianity as it is founded on and remains faithful to the "evangel"—the good news of Jesus Christ. It is not unusual to see the term *evangelical* used in documents of the Roman Catholic Church and almost all so-called mainline Protestant denominations to denote the message of the incarnation of God in Jesus Christ, God's love for humanity demonstrated in Christ's death and resurrection, and especially salvation by God's grace alone apart from human achievements. In this sense, then, evangelical is contrasted with moralistic or legalistic religion; evangelicalism is the Christian movement proclaiming the good news that human persons can be saved by receiving a free gift won for them by Jesus Christ in his death and resurrection.

The second historical use of *evangelical* derives from the Protestant Reformation of the sixteenth century. In parts of Europe dominated by Protestant state churches rooted in the reforming works of Martin Luther, Ulrich Zwingli, and John Calvin in the sixteenth century, *evangelical* is simply synonymous with *Protestant*. While traveling around Germany, Switzerland, and portions of eastern France, for example, one may see many churches labeled simply "evangelical" and know they are Protestant without knowing precisely which Protestant traditions they represent. Lutherans especially like to use the term *evangelical* in the names of their churches and denominations; some Reformed (Calvinist) churches also use it. In the United States this use of the term appears in the name of the largest Lutheran denomination—the Evangelical Lutheran Church in America—which is a union of two previously existing Lutheran synods or denominations in the U.S. The architects of the union consciously chose to incorporate the word *evangelical* into the name of the new denomination in order to state publicly that it would be gospel-centered in the Lutheran sense of proclaiming the doctrine of salvation by grace through faith alone.

The third definition of *evangelical* is tied to the British context of the Church of England, which is sometimes called Anglican. In the United States it is known as the Episcopal Church. The Church of England, though doctrinally Protestant since the time of Elizabeth I in the sixteenth century, has also always contained different and sometimes conflicting parties. The evangelical party within the Church of England is not organized, but it is composed of those priests and bishops and lay members who seek to "Protestantize" Anglicanism and who resist the party that would retrieve and strengthen Roman Catholic elements within the church's history and liturgy. The evangelicals tend to be "low church" in that they reduce the liturgical aspects of worship to a minimum, stress the priesthood of all believers (without discarding the ministerial office), and emphasize the necessity of personal faith in Jesus Christ for salvation (as opposed to baptismal regeneration). The evangelicals within the worldwide Anglican/Church of England/Episcopal communion look back to the first-generation reformers of the English church under Henry VIII in the mid-sixteenth century, most of whom were martyred by his Catholic daughter Mary Tudor ("Bloody Mary") for their enthusiastic Protestant zeal.

The fourth distinct use of *evangelical* arises out of the Pietist and revivalist attempts to reform and revive Protestant Christianity in Germany, Great Britain, and North America in the early eighteenth century. At a time when the state churches and even most of the so-called sects (dissenting denominations) had fallen into a state of spiritual lethargy described as "dead orthodoxy" by the "enthusiasts" (spiritual reformers), the latter broke on the scene to enliven Protestant Christianity with a greater sense of spiritual fervor and vitality. In Germany this movement of "heart Christianity" that came to be known as Pietism emphasized the necessity of personal conversion to Jesus Christ through repentance and faith, a life of devotion through Bible reading and study, prayer and worship, and holiness of life. The Pietists often met in conventicles or small groups outside the formal structure of the state churches and were sometimes persecuted as a result. Lutheran leaders such as Philip Spener and August Francke firmly established a spiritual renewal movement within the state church; Count von Zinzendorf turned a small band of wandering spiritual Christians known as the Moravian Brethren into an influential renewal movement within Protestant Christianity.

In Great Britain and the American colonies a revival known as the Great Awakening broke out under the leadership of John and Charles Wesley, their friend George Whitefield, and Puritan preacher Jonathan Edwards. Those who embraced these "new measures" of Christianity that tended toward emotion and appeal for personal decision for Christ called themselves evangelicals. Thus, in the second half of the eighteenth century and into the nineteenth century in Great Britain and North America, evangelical was virtually synonymous with Great Awakening-inspired revivalism. Evangelicals rejected sacramental salvation and covenant salvation as inadequate views of true conversion to Christ and urged all people—baptized and born "in the covenant" (i.e., into Christian homes and churches), as well as those entirely outside the church's embrace—to repent and believe in Jesus Christ for the remission (forgiveness) of sins and for transformation of life (regeneration).

The fifth definition of *evangelical* comes from the conservative Protestant reaction to the rise of liberal Protestantism in the nineteenth and early twentieth centuries. It is nearly synonymous with fundamentalism—at least as that term was originally used and understood. Conservative Protestants who wished to reaffirm what they considered the "fundamentals of the faith"—such as a supernatural worldview (including the miracles of the Bible), the transcendence of God, the reality of the Trinity, the deity of Jesus Christ, the virgin birth and bodily resurrection of Jesus, and the inspiration and authority of the Bible—called themselves both fundamentalists and evangelicals. Many of their leading thinkers, speakers, and writers stood in the Reformed Protestant tradition and looked back to the great Protestant orthodox thinkers such as Francis Turretin, Archibald Alexander, and Charles Hodge for guidance and inspiration. The paradigm of such a fundamentalist evangelical was Presbyterian scholar J. Gresham Machen, who taught at Princeton Seminary and then helped found Westminster Theological Seminary in Philadelphia to rival Princeton as it allegedly declined into modernistic Bible scholarship and theology around the beginning of the twentieth century. The early twentieth-century fundamentalists (especially before 1925) were by and large simply defenders of Protestant orthodoxy with a somewhat militant attitude toward fighting the encroachments of revisionist Protestantism. *Evangelical* was one of the terms used to identify them. After 1925, the year of the infamous Scopes evolution trial in Tennessee, fundamentalism gradually began to withdraw from the mainstream of denominational Protestantism into its own subculture, with a plethora of newly founded Bible schools, publishing houses, denominations, conventions, and missionary agencies.

The sixth use of *evangelical* is the one that provides at least the beginning point and center of this handbook and its subject matter. In the 1940s and 1950s postfundamentalist evangelicalism began to break away from the increasingly militant and separatistic fundamentalism of the 1920s and 1930s. There is no absolute line dividing the older fundamentalism from the newer evangelicalism, and matters are especially confused by the fact that nearly all fundamentalists—no matter how militant and separatistic—have continued to call themselves evangelicals. Most postfundamentalist evangelicals do not wish to be called fundamentalists, even though their basic theological orientation is not very different (in most cases, at least) from that of the early fundamentalists such as J. Gresham Machen. The new, postfundamentalist evangelicals were derisively labeled "neo-evangelicals" by their more militant and separatistic cousins, who accused them of accommodating to the secular spirit of the age and to liberal-modernistic Protestantism. Postfundamentalist evangelicals wanted to be known simply as evangelicals and asserted that there was an evangelical heritage that was greater than fundamentalism. They appealed to prefundamentalist evangelicals such as the Pietist-revivalist leaders and thinkers of the Great Awakening and to the great theologians of Protestant orthodoxy, and they sought to engage evangelical belief and experience with contemporary society and issues in a less negative way than militant fundamentalists. During the crucial decades of the 1940s and 1950s postfundamentalist evangelicals formed a strong multidenominational coalition in Britain and America and created a large and broad network of cooperating organizations to renew conservative, revivalist Christianity and spread its influence in Western society. In the United States the National Association of Evangelicals (NAE) was formed to provide an alternative to the liberal-dominated Federal Council of Churches; eventually over fifty conservative Protestant denominations with at least some sympathy with revivalism (e.g., Billy Graham's evangelistic ministry) joined. One motto of the NAE became the old Pietist saying "In essentials unity, in nonessentials liberty, in all things charity."

The seventh definition of *evangelical* and *evangelicalism* is popular rather than scholarly or historical. One often hears or reads the adjective *evangelical* used by journalists to describe anyone or any group that seems particularly (by the journalist's standards) enthusiastic, aggressive, fanatical, or even simply missionary-minded. True fundamentalists (militant, separatistic, ultraconservative Protestants) are often described in the media as evangelical; sometimes Roman Catholic missionaries and even Muslim groups that engage in missionary endeavors are labeled evangelical by journalists. This seventh use cannot simply be rejected; it has caught on in contemporary language. Jehovah's Witnesses, considered a cult by many conservative Protestants, are often called evangelical simply because of their door-to-door witnessing techniques. However, for the purpose of this handbook, this journalistic and popular use of *evangelical* will be ignored.

Like many good terms and categories, then, *evangelical* and *evangelicalism* have a broad semantic range, one that is so variegated that the terms seem to lose all shape. It is tempting even for evangelicals at times to give up the label. However, it should be remembered that many other religious labels for movements and categories for theological orientations suffer the same vagueness and contested nature as *evangelicalism*. Exactly what is Reformed Christianity and Reformed theology? Beyond the fact that it is a tradition rooted in the theological contributions of sixteenth-century reformers Martin Bucer, Ulrich Zwingli, and John Calvin, there is little consensus even among those who call themselves Reformed. Can anyone precisely define the charismatic movement? Who is a charismatic; what makes a person truly charismatic? What is liberal Protestant

Christianity? These and many other good and useful and even necessary labels and categories are notoriously difficult to pin down, and yet they continue to be used by scholars and lay people alike. Each one does refer to some phenomenon—a tradition-community that may be bewilderingly diverse and yet at the same time somewhat united in contrast to other tradition-communities.

Our approach to describing evangelicalism—which is the context within which evangelical theology functions—will be historical; here we will attempt to define by telling a story. It is the story of the rise of postfundamentalist evangelicalism—its roots, crucible, birth, and contemporary existence. The focus of our story will be theology—the distinctive ideas about authority for religious belief, revelation and Scripture, God and Jesus Christ, salvation, and so forth. However, the story of theology is never the narrative of pure ideas falling out of the sky. evangelicalism is a tradition-community, and evangelical theology is its peculiar recipe of religious commitments, values, and beliefs. Before delving into the background history of evangelicalism, it will be helpful to set forth at least a tentative definition of the category and of evangelical theology. The perceptive reader will recognize immediately that the definitions set forth here draw together several of the seven definitions of *evangelical* outlined above.

Evangelicalism is a loose affiliation (coalition, network, mosaic, patchwork, family) of mostly Protestant Christians of many orthodox (Trinitarian) denominations and independent churches and parachurch organizations that affirm a supernatural worldview; the unsurpassable authority of the Bible for all matters of faith and religious practice; Jesus Christ as unique Lord, God, and Savior; the fallenness of humanity and salvation provided by Jesus Christ through his suffering, death, and resurrection; the necessity of personal repentance and faith (conversion) for full salvation; the importance of a devotional life and growth in holiness and discipleship; the urgency of gospel evangelism and social transformation; and the return of Jesus Christ to judge the world and establish the final, full rule and reign of God. Many evangelicals affirm more; none affirm less or deny any of these basic belief commitments. The genius of evangelicalism is its combination of orthodox Protestantism, conservative revivalism, and transdenominational ecumenism. Within it coexist and cooperate peacefully (most of the time) Protestants committed to competing secondary doctrines: predestination, free will, premillennialism, amillennialism, infant baptism, believer baptism, pouring, immersion, literal creationism, theistic evolution. Occasionally, of course, and perhaps increasingly, evangelicals of differing doctrinal persuasions with regard to secondary doctrines (denominational distinctives) fight with each other. The old Calvinist versus Arminian (predestination versus free will) argument erupts from time to time and threatens to disrupt the uneasy unity of evangelicalism. The powerfully unifying figure of evangelist Billy Graham has helped keep the evangelical community together in cooperation in spite of such differences. What will happen when the "Graham glue" dissolves with his passing (or passing the torch) is a favorite subject of speculation among evangelical-watchers.

Another way of describing evangelicalism is by saying that it is a movement for the renewal of Protestant Christianity. It shares with the Protestant Reformers and classical Protestantism in general basic Christian beliefs about the Scriptures, God, Jesus Christ, and salvation, but it regards classic, historic Protestant Christianity as needing reform. Thus, evangelicalism represents a reform of the Reformation. Evangelical reform has a program that centers around *retrieval, restoration, revival,* and *relevance.* Evangelicals have always wanted to retrieve the original impulses of Christianity as they are revealed in the New Testament and early church documents as well as the ideals of the Protestant Reformers. This retrieval is necessary because of the occasional declensions of Protestantism from these original impulses. Evangelicals have often decried a condition they call "dead orthodoxy" in the churches, a condition in which church leaders and members confess correct doctrine but show little or no evidence of personal experience of the transforming presence and power of God. They have also criticized the modern deviations from historic Christianity known as "neo-Protestantism" or liberal modernism. In order to challenge and correct these diseases in Protestantism, evangelicals have sought to recover both basic Christian doctrine and the New Testament and original Protestant experiences of God's transforming power in people's lives.

Not only have evangelicals sought to renew Protestant Christianity through retrieval, they have also sought to restore the spirit of early Christianity within the churches. While they may differ about the details of this restoration, all evangelicals firmly believe that contemporary Christianity is authentic to the extent that it reflects the heart of the apostolic Christian movement as that appears in the New Testament. The missionary journeys of Paul, for example, form a favorite theme of evangelical preaching and teaching, and evangelicals believe that missionary and evangelistic endeavor is just as important for authentic Christianity today as it was in the first century. Most evangelicals would not go so far as to declare the entire church between the New Testament and the rise of evangelicalism apostate, but many would consider it seriously defective and in dire need of renewal and revival. Many evangelicals, then, view evangelical revivalism and conservative Christian theology and proclamation at least a partial restoration of the "true Christianity" that declined into partial obscurity for centuries after the deaths of the apostles.

Thus, crucial to the renewal of Christianity that evangelicals envision is revival. Revival does not necessarily connote emotional responses to emotional preaching. That has, of course, been a feature of some of evangelicalism. But more important to true revival for most evangelicals is heartfelt, passionate appeals for personal appropriation of God's grace in Jesus Christ and his cross through repentance and faith and a "daily, personal relationship with Jesus Christ" through prayer and Bible reading. Evangelicals have always suspected that authentic Christianity involves the affections and will as much as, if not more than, the intellect. Evangelical revival appeals to religious affections and calls for people to make personal decisions for and lifelong commitments to Jesus Christ. Many evangelical churches have institutionalized revival by holding special "protracted meetings" over several days or even weeks. These were called "Holy Fairs" in seventeenth-century Scotland; in twentieth-century North America they were sometimes referred to as Jesus festivals. Everyone is familiar with the Billy Graham crusades. But whatever they are called, evangelicals of all kinds initiate spiritual renewal events that seek to breathe new life into individuals and churches.

Finally, evangelicalism seeks renewal of Christianity through relevance. Evangelicals have in varying degrees emphasized the importance of contextualizing the Christian message and relating it to contemporary problems and issues. They criticize and seek to avoid real accommodation to culture, while at the same time translating the gospel into cultural idioms, using contemporary means of communication in order to facilitate retrieval, restoration, and revival. The "new measures" used by the revival preachers of the first and second Great Awakenings of the eighteenth and nineteenth centuries give examples of this evangelical interest in renewal through relevance. During the Great Awakenings those churches that cooperated with itinerant, circuit-riding preachers and produced sermons and used illustrations that related to the everyday lives of people in the colonies and along the frontiers grew, while those that resisted such new measures and insisted on sticking to old language and methods tended to lose members. Evangelicalism has not usually been noted for its relevance, but that is no doubt because of its reaction against liberal Christianity's (neo-Protestantism's) attempts to accommodate the biblical and historic Christian message to the everchanging climates of contemporary cultures. Evangelicals seek to retain the original biblical message, as they understand it, while communicating it in contemporary ways using modern means. Above all, they seek to appeal to the personal spiritual needs of individuals in their everyday lives—needs for release from anxiety of guilt, acceptance within a community of true believers, and hope for a better future, even if only after this life.

Evangelical theology is, most simply, that theological scholarship done within the context of the evangelical movement for renewal of historic Protestant Christianity. The postfundamentalist evangelical coalition contains several publishing houses and publications as well as professional theological societies, and there is a sense in which any theological reflection published, read, or widely discussed within these is evangelical theology. That is, of course, a descriptive approach to defining evangelical theology. What about a prescriptive approach? Are there boundaries of evangelical theology? How might one determine whether a particular book or article or scholarly paper that is published or read within evangelicalism by a self-identified evangelical theologian truly is evangelical? If *evangelical* is compatible with anything and everything, it is literally meaningless. Identifying either a controlling center or limiting boundaries of authentically evangelical theology is notoriously dangerous; others are bound to disagree most strongly.

Our approach is to use history as the guide. Rather than setting boundaries and examining every theological contribution by a predetermined set of rigid criteria, we prefer to look at each contribution through the lens of the history of evangelical Christianity, which has always contained a strong reforming and reshaping impulse within itself. In other words, evangelicalism is dynamic rather than static. Just because something is new does not automatically mean it is not evangelical. However, evangelicalism's history does have a unifying ethos as described above—a strong, gravitational center that holds it together. This can take many new shapes, and it can be expressed and interpreted in different ways. Evangelical theology, then, is that form of mostly Protestant Christian reflection on God and salvation (etc.) that is guided by the ultimate authority of Scripture, acknowledges that God is supremely revealed in Jesus Christ, and includes a strong focus on personal salvation by repentance and faith. More could be included, of course, but this brief definition is sufficient to give some shape to evangelical theology. It is not any and all Protestant theological reflection and formulation. Liberal theology that is characterized by "maximal acknowledgment of the claims of modernity" is not compatible with evangelical theology. Nor is all Protestant orthodoxy; in order to count as evangelical, it would have to include affirmation of and reflection on "conversional piety"—the dimension of salvation dear to the hearts of all evangelicals in which persons come to know God as Savior only through a personal relationship with Jesus Christ that begins with, or at least comes to full fruition in, conscious repentance and trust.

Evangelicalism and evangelical theology cross denominational and confessional boundaries; one can find evangelicals and evangelical theologians in many Protestant traditions and communities. One of the most influential evangelical theologians of the later decades of the twentieth century and early years of the twenty-first century is Donald G. Bloesch, who taught theology for many years at a mainline Presbyterian seminary (University of Dubuque Theological Seminary) and maintained membership and ministerial ordination in the mainline Protestant United Church of Christ. Bloesch's definitions and descriptions of evangelical express the category's unity and diversity and continuity and discontinuity with fundamentalism:

> "Evangelical" can therefore be said to indicate a particular thrust or emphasis within the church, namely, that which upholds the gospel of free grace as we see this in Jesus Christ. An evangelical will consequently be Christocentric and not merely theocentric (as are the deists and a great many mystics). Yet it is not the teachings of Jesus Christ that are considered of paramount importance but his sacrificial life and death on the cross of Calvary. The evangel is none other than the meaning of the cross.[2]
>
> Evangelicalism unashamedly stands for the fundamentals of the historic faith, but as a movement it transcends and corrects the defensive, sectarian mentality commonly associated with Fundamentalism. Though many, perhaps most, fundamentalists are evangelicals, evangelical Christianity is wider and deeper than Fundamentalism, which is basically a movement of reaction in the churches in this period of history. Evangelicalism in the classical sense fulfills the basic goals and aspirations of Fundamentalism but rejects the ways in which these goals are realized.[3]

According to Bloesch and many other commentators on evangelical history and theology, then, evangelicalism is a broad and diverse movement that includes within itself many (but not all) Lutherans, Reformed Protestants (i.e., "Calvinists"), Wesleyans, Baptists, Pentecostals, and adherents of other

---

[2]Donald G. Bloesch, *The Future of Evangelical Christianity* (Garden City, NY: Doubleday, 1983), 15.
[3]Ibid., 22.

Protestant traditions. It also includes many fundamentalists, although Bloesch is reluctant to identify evangelicalism with fundamentalism because of their different mind-sets and approaches to culture, other Christians, higher education, and a variety of other subjects. Some evangelical spokespersons define and describe evangelicalism and evangelical theology more restrictively than Bloesch. Those who value evangelicalism's fundamentalist roots tend to limit it to people and organizations that affirm biblical inerrancy. Others who especially value evangelicalism's Pietist and revivalist roots tend to limit it to people and organizations that affirm radical conversion as the only true initiation into Christian existence and who reject infant baptism as a sacrament. A few evangelicals would argue that authentic evangelicalism is limited to those who believe in the classical Calvinist doctrines of unconditional election and irresistible grace. However, the majority of evangelicals and scholarly commentators on evangelicalism emphasize its diversity as well as its unity; the genius of postfundamentalist evangelicalism and evangelical theology is its ability to embrace a variety of confessional and liturgical differences within a unifying framework of belief and experience.

2

The Roots of
Evangelical Theology
in Pietism

Was there a first evangelical theologian or first volume of evangelical theology? Probably not. Instead of identifying a definite beginning of Evangelicalism or evangelical theology, we should explore the distant roots of postfundamentalist Evangelicalism in several movements to reform Protestantism in Europe, Great Britain, and North America. In other words, the story of post-World War II postfundamentalist Evangelicalism and its theology begins three hundred years earlier with a general rise of spiritual fervor and a renaissance of biblical theology among Protestants that has come to be known vaguely as Pietism.

The Pietist movement began among German Lutherans in the late seventeenth cenutury and quickly spread to Scandinavia. It influenced Great Britain through Puritans who were influenced by Pietism and through John and Charles Wesley, the founders of the Methodist movement. It was brought to the American colonies by leading Pietists such as Count Nikolaus von Zinzendorf and his Moravian followers, as well as by other groups of "heart Christians" who often called themselves Brethren. The ethos of Pietism is well described by F. Ernest Stoeffler: "Wherever it is found its ethos is manifested in a religious self-understanding which the author has characterized elsewhere as experiential, biblical, perfectionistic, and oppositive."[1] In other words, Pietists are always concerned that Christianity be something more than historical knowledge and mental assent to doctrines; they want to distinguish authentic Christianity from false or merely nominal Christianity by identifying the "real thing" by life-transforming experience of God in conversion and devotion to God in the "inner man" and by discipleship that is shaped by the Bible, aims towards perfection, and seeks to be "in the world but not of the world."

The Pietist movement is usually thought to have begun with the publication of a book entitled *Pia Desideria* (Pious desires) by German Lutheran minister Philip Spener (1635–1705) in 1675. Spener, a highly regarded and influential minister of the Lutheran state church of Prussia, was concerned that true Christianity was being replaced by dead orthodoxy, ritualism, and legalism. His understanding of "true Christianity" was greatly influenced by his godly mother and by her favorite devotional book, *True Christianity,* by Protestant mystic and spiritual writer Johann Arndt (1555–1621). Spener, following Arndt, defined true Christianity in contrast with the conventional orthodoxy of the state church with reference to the "inner man." That is, according to Spener and later Pietists, each person has within himself or herself a spiritual organ sometimes loosely called "the heart" that is the core of personality

---

[1]F. Ernest Stoeffler, ed., *Continental Pietism and Early American Christianity* (Grand Rapids: Wm. B. Eerdmans, 1976), 9.

and seat of governing affections. This inner man is the locus of God's work in conversion and regeneration, and each person who becomes a true Christian experiences a transformation there. Such a transformation, which later evangelicals commonly came to call being "born again," transcends intellect and will; through it the person who repents and trusts in Christ for salvation receives "the expulsive power of a new affection" that inclines him or her to have a taste for the things of God and turn away from desires of the "world, flesh and devil." Spener returned repeatedly to this basic theme of the inner man, and it became, in various permutations, the constant leitmotif of Pietism and later Evangelicalism:

> One should therefore emphasize that the divine means of Word and sacrament are concerned with the inner man. Hence it is not enough that we hear the Word with our outward ear, but we must let it penetrate to our heart, so that we may hear the Holy Spirit speak there, that is, with vibrant emotion and comfort feel the sealing of the Spirit and the power of the Word. Nor is it enough to be baptized, but the inner man, where we have put on Christ in Baptism, must also keep Christ on and bear witness to him in our outward life. Nor is it enough to have received the Lord's Supper externally, but the inner man must truly be fed with that blessed food. Nor is it enough to pray outwardly with our mouth, but true prayer, and the best prayer, occurs in the inner man, and it either breaks forth in words or remains in the soul, yet God will find and hit upon it. Nor, again, is it enough to worship God in an external temple, but the inner man worships God best in his own temple, whether or not he is in an external temple at the time.[2]

---

[2]Philip Jacob Spener, *Pia Desideria,* trans. Theodore G. Tappert (Philadelphia: Fortress Press, 1964), 117.

Spener organized conventicles (small groups) of "heart Christians" in his parish in Frankfurt, and from there the "conventicle movement" (original Pietism) spread throughout Lutheran and Reformed churches in Europe. The conventicles were to be spiritual renewal groups under the auspices of trained, Pietist clergymen, but they quickly evolved into home meetings of "Bible readers" outside the authority of church and state. In many parts of Europe these groups were persecuted, and some of them emigrated to North America to find religious freedom. There they organized new denominations of "free churches" composed of "true Christians." Some became Baptists under the influence of Baptist missionaries. Some remained independent of any particular tradition. Denominations in the United States such as the Church of the Brethren, the Baptist General Conference (formerly the Swedish Baptist Conference), the Evangelical Free Church of America, and the Evangelical Covenant Church of America all evolved out of the European Pietist movement begun by Spener. While these and other Pietist-evangelical groups disagree about specific practices such as baptism and church government, they agree that authentic Christian existence begins with conversion to Jesus Christ by the Spirit of God within the inner man (heart, soul, inward being) and that it always involves heartfelt repentance and faith (trust) in Jesus Christ. Furthermore, they emphasize a semimystical "daily relationship with Christ" that flows out of that initial conversion experience. Some commentators on Pietism-Evangelicalism have labeled this distinctive evangelical spirituality "conversional piety." In traditional theological terms this distinctive Pietist and evangelical ethos may be described as an elevation of regeneration and sanctification over or alongside justification. Critics have labeled it "decisionism" and decried its perceived subjective emphasis.

In spite of his emphasis on the inner man and inward spiritual transformation, Spener was not a true mystic or subjectivist. He was most certainly not a religious fanatic (except to some of his harshest critics). Throughout *Pia Desideria* and other writings he strove to balance biblical authority, confessional fidelity, and theological scholarship with experience of God in the inner man. He did not reject either side of this equation and insisted that "head" and "heart" be held in complementary relationship. Clearly, however, he perceived the greater danger as that of rejecting or neglecting heart Christianity, which led later Pietists to coin the motto "Better a live heresy than a dead orthodoxy!" This was clearly intended as hyperbole. Spener advocated spiritual training for ministerial students and argued against merely educating them in orthodoxy and theological polemics. He railed against corruption in government, society, and church and laid out a program for reforming Protestantism through rigorous examination of the character and spiritual lives of ministerial candidates. He preached boldly against princes and magistrates who neglected church attendance and called for renewal, revival, and reform in all areas of public and private life. Typical of his advice to ministers and students is this exhortation in *Pia Desideria*:

> Let us remember that in the last judgment we shall not be asked how learned we were and whether we displayed our learning before the world; to what extent we enjoyed the favor of men and knew how to keep it; with what honors we were exalted and how great a reputation in the world we left behind us; or how many treasures of earthly goods we amassed for our children and thereby drew a curse upon ourselves. Instead, we shall be asked how faithfully and with how childlike a heart we sought to further the kingdom of God; with how pure and godly a teaching and how worthy an example we tried to edify our hearers amid the scorn of the world, denial of self,

taking up of the cross, and imitation of our Savior; with what zeal we opposed not only error but also wickedness of life; or with what constancy and cheerfulness we endured the persecution or adversity thrust upon us by the manifestly godless world or by false brethren, and amid such suffering praised our God.[3]

Contrary to what one might think, Spener and other early Pietist leaders were not at all fanatical, overly emotional, or anti-intellectual. Nor did they depart from basic Protestant doctrinal orthodoxy. In fact, they expressed nothing but the highest praise for Luther and quoted him often; those who were of the Reformed heritage revered Calvin and affirmed the classical Reformed confessions of faith. Spener and those who followed him simply believed that the Reformation was unfinished and that the heirs of Luther and Calvin had fallen into a stale, overly intellectualized and polemical religion that lacked life and power. Of course, the Pietists were accused of heresy by their critics within the state churches of Europe. They were labeled "enthusiasts," which was at that time virtually a synonym for "religious fanatics." As noted earlier, some of them were hounded and persecuted by civil authorities at the behest of religious leaders. In many places it was illegal to meet for Bible study and discussion and for prayer without benefit of clergy. Nevertheless, the Pietist movement grew very quickly, and its influence spread into all corners of Protestant Europe in the early eighteenth century. Some church historians have labeled it "the second Reformation" and many have come to regard it as the beginning of what is now known as Evangelicalism.

Two other early leaders of Pietism deserve mention in this brief account of the history and theology of Evangelicalism. They are August Hermann Francke (1663–1727) and Count Nikolas Ludwig von Zinzendorf (1700–1760). Francke was raised

[3]Spener, 36-37.

in a home and church deeply imbued with Spener's Pietist influence. Spener eventually became his teacher and mentor in Leipzig, where Spener was court preacher to the prince of Saxony and Francke was a student. Francke was studying to be a minister and yet doubted his own salvation because he had not experienced the regenerating power of God in the inner man. One night before he was to preach, the young student minister fell on his knees and asked God for such a heart-changing and assuring experience. According to his own testimony he endured a protracted *Busskampf* or "struggle of repentance" with tears and crying out to God before receiving the sought-after assurance. This became a model for true initiation into authentic Christianity for many Pietists and later evangelicals. Francke helped found the first Pietist university at Halle in Germany, and in the same city he established and led a variety of charitable institutions including free schools, an orphanage, a hospital, and a publishing house. From Halle, Francke also sent out missionaries to India and other countries that had previously been virtually ignored by Protestants. Like Spener before him, Francke was a devout Lutheran (within a united Lutheran and Reformed state church) who never questioned the classical Protestant doctrines of biblical authority and justification by grace through faith alone. Also like Spener, however, Francke believed that one could participate in the sacraments and learn the catechism and even assent to correct doctrine and not be saved. That was his own story. What made the difference between the two conditions? For Francke and Pietism in general, it was the experience of *Busskampf*—struggle of repentance and the life of Christ dwelling in the inner man that flowed from it. Francke added to the stream of Pietism and early Evangelicalism a passion for missions and world evangelism, as well as concern for the poor and disadvantaged. Under his leadership the city of Halle became a great center of Christian education, social work, publishing, and missionary endeavor.

Zinzendorf has been described somewhat tongue in cheek as the "noble Jesus freak." He was a member of the German nobility and quite eccentric, as well as passionate about Jesus. Spener was his godfather; Francke was his mentor. As a child and adolescent he seemed to have an inordinate obsession with matters spiritual. The young count became disillusioned with the spiritual aridity of the state church of Saxony and allowed a roving band of Moravian Christian pilgrims to settle on his estate at Berthelsdorf that he renamed Herrnhut—"the Lord's Watch." The Moravians were spiritual descendents of Jan Hus, the forerunner of the Protestant Reformation in Prague (Bohemia), who was burned at the stake by the Catholic Council of Constance about a century before Luther's Reformation divided the church. They had existed as a separate Protestant body within a predominantly Catholic country for two centuries before some left it and found refuge on Zinzendorf's land. The count joined their church and became their bishop; they became a semi-autonomous branch of the Lutheran church of Germany. Although small in number, the Moravians exercised tremendous influence within the burgeoning Pietist movement in Europe. They sent missionaries to many places including South Africa, Labrador, and the Caribbean as well as the North American colonies. They founded a chapel in London where John Wesley's heart was "strangely warmed," and afterwards Wesley lived among them in Germany for a time. They began traditions such as New Year's Eve prayer vigils ("watchnight services") and Easter morning sunrise services that entered into the stream of evangelical Christianity. Their worship was intense, although not particularly loud or overly emotional, and Zinzendorf and the Moravians emphasized inward experience of Jesus Christ as crucified and risen Savior ("personal Savior and Lord") over precise doctrinal knowledge and assent. As with Spener and Francke, however, this did not mean they discarded doctrine. Rather, they heartily affirmed the basic confessional statements of Lutheranism. Nevertheless, Zinzendorf and the Moravians held in highest esteem a semimystical experience that is devoid of concepts and ushers one into authentic Christian existence. In a lecture entitled "On the Essential Character and Circumstance of the Life of a Christian" delivered at the Moravian Brethren chapel in London, Zinzendorf attempted to explain the nature of this experience and the life with Christ into which it leads. The beginning of Christianity is when the crucified Savior Jesus "appears and looks into the heart" of a person, which can happen at any moment but most often happens when a sermon is preached or a hymn is sung:

> He who in this moment, in this instant, when the Saviour appears to him and when He says to him, as to Peter, "Do you love me in this figure?"—he who can say, "You know all things; you know that I love you"; he who in this minute, in this instant, goes over to Him with his heart, passes into Him, and loses himself in His tormented form and suffering figure—he remains in Him eternally, without interruption, through all eons; he can no longer be estranged from Him. . . . Then our perdition is at an end; then flesh and blood have lost. Satan, who had already lost his case in court, really lays no more claim on such a soul; and it is just as if a man, who had sold himself to Satan, gets back his promissory note, as if the slip of paper came flying into the meeting, torn to pieces. The signature, the note, says the apostle, is torn up and fastened to the cross, pounded through with nails, and forever cancelled; and this is registered at the same time, that is, we are set free; we are legally acquitted. When the books are opened, so it will be found.[4]

---

[4]Nicholaus Ludwig Count von Zinzendorf, *Nine Public Lectures on Important Subjects in Religion,* trans. George W. Forell (Eugene, OR: Wipf & Stock Publishers, 1998), 83-84.

This statement of conversion nicely illustrates, in admittedly flowery and somewhat eccentric language, the Pietistic and evangelical doctrine of salvation: it is an experience of Jesus Christ in which Christ encounters a person, calls him or her to respond in love (which necessarily includes repentance and trust), whereupon Christ enters the person's heart (Spener's inner man) and unites with him or her. This is at once justification (forgiveness and imputed righteousness) and regeneration (cleansing from corruption of sin and impartation of the Holy Spirit). Of course, Spener, Francke, and Zinzendorf all believed, like many evangelicals past and present, that this transforming experience, which happens in a moment, may be preceded by a process of preparation that begins with infant baptism and continues through Christian nurture; but they rejected any idea that persons can be truly saved and enter into authentic Christian life without this kind of conversion experience.

Pietism was the original Protestant renewal movement, and it did manage to revive large portions of European, British, and North American Protestantism in the eighteenth century. It assumed the truth and authority of the Bible and the major Christian creeds, such as the Nicene Creed and the basic Protestant confessional statements like the Augsburg Confession (Lutheran) and Heidelberg Confession and Catechism (Reformed), but it sought to add to objective truth the dimension of subjective, inward experience. It moved the standard for authentic Christianity beyond baptism and doctrinal belief to include genuine conversion to Christ through repentance and faith and a life of visible Christianity. For this it was widely denounced by defenders of confessional orthodoxy and the status quo in the state churches as divisive, sectarian, superspiritual, spiritually proud, and fanatical. The basic ethos of Pietism set the mood and course for all Evangelicalism; post-World War II postfundamentalist Evangelicalism is Pietism's heir, even though it also often looks back to Pietism's enemies among the Protestant scholastic theologians with great respect and reverence. This is the pathos of modern Evangelicalism: its dual heritage. It was born in Pietism, but it has always flirted with rationalistic, scholastic Protestant orthodoxy. From Pietism evangelical theology inherits its fascination with soteriology—the doctrine of salvation. If Evangelicalism and evangelical theology are about anything, they are about the meaning of true salvation and authentic Christianity, defined in terms of the experience of salvation. At the same time, clearly modern Evangelicalism and evangelical theology are also heirs of Protestant orthodoxy, with its precise definitions of doctrinal correctness and polemical arguments over the fine points of dogma. While these are not necessarily conflictual, they do often fall into some tension with each other.

3

The Revivalist
Roots of Evangelical
Theology

Following closely upon the heels of Pietism was the revivalist movement, which also profoundly impacted Evangelicalism and evangelical theology. Revivalism was the phenomenon in Great Britain and North America that saw emotional preaching calling masses of mostly already baptized people, often outdoors, to make decisions to repent and follow Jesus Christ. It began with three ministers of traditional Protestant denominations and swept through the English-speaking world and from there to the whole world. The three eighteenth-century founders of revivalism were John Wesley, George Whitefield, and Jonathan Edwards. Their numerous followers and imitators include Charles G. Finney, Dwight L. Moody, Billy Sunday, Aimee Semple McPherson, and Billy Graham. Unlike some of their spiritual descendants, Wesley, Whitefield, and Edwards were highly educated clergy and scholars in biblical and theological studies. They were not merely religious entrepreneurs seeking a following. They were faithful sons of their Protestant traditions who happened to be deeply influenced by versions of Pietism. Edwards, of course, was also a Puritan, and through him and his influence the Puritan tradition entered into the stream of evangelical life and thought.

None of these early revivalist leaders of the so-called Great Awakening (1730s and 1740s) envisioned a departure from or split within their respective Protestant churches. That became inevitable when the leaders of those denominations (Anglican/Episcopalian and Congregational/Presbyterian) refused to support the revival fires that burned where the revivalists preached. Wesley, Whitefield, and Edwards, however, unanimously and sincerely affirmed the basic doctrines of historic Christian orthodoxy (as expressed for example in the Nicene Creed) and of Protestant orthodoxy (as expressed in their denominational statements of faith such as the Westminster Confession and Catechism and the Church of England's Thirty-Nine Articles of Religion). Like the Pietists of Europe, they believed that "head knowledge" and "historical faith" must be distinguished from "heart knowledge" and "inward faith" and that the latter are what distinguishes true Christianity from nominal Christianity. The revivalists simply went a step beyond the Pietists and proclaimed the need for each person publicly to repent and receive Jesus Christ by an act of inward faith as well as outward profession. They firmly believed that the gospel they proclaimed and the "new measures" they used to proclaim it could facilitate radical spiritual transformations in individuals and societies.

Nothing quite like the Great Awakening of 1739–42 had ever happened in Christianity—at least not since the days of the apostles. Church of England minister John Wesley (1703–91) and his brother Charles (1707–88) had founded something called "the Holy Club" by its detractors at Oxford University when they were students. Their friend George White-field (1714–70), who also later became a minister of the Church of England, was a member of the club. Much later these three friends all had experiences that led them beyond the striving for holiness through strict spiritual disciplines that brought on them the appellation Holy Club and caused them to accept and proclaim the Pietist doctrine of salvation. John Wesley struggled with doubts about his salvation even as a priest of the state church and was not freed from doubt until his heart was "strangely warmed" during a service at the Moravian Brethren chapel in Aldersgate Street in London. Eventually, the three friends began and cooperated together in an evangelistic venture that included open-air preaching throughout England. Whitefield traveled to the American colonies and preached to large numbers of people in cities such as Philadelphia, where he was "puffed" by journalist Benjamin Franklin. Among the "new measures" used by these revivalists and those who joined with them was vivid description of the consequences of neglecting repentance and conversion. Whitefield especially was both criticized and applauded for his rhetorical flourishes that resulted in thousands of emotional responses. He loudly described to his mass of eager listeners the feelings of a person who has died without repenting and accepting Christ:

> O wretched Man that I am, who shall deliver me from the Body of Death! Are all the Grand Deceiver's inviting Promises come to this? O Damned Apostate! Oh that I had never hearkened to his beguiling Insinuations! Oh that I had rejected his very first Suggestions with the utmost Detestation and Abhorrence! Oh that I had taken up my cross and followed Christ! But alas! These reflections come now too late. But must I live for ever tormented in these Flames? Oh, Eternity! That thought fills

me with Despair. I cannot, will not, yet I must be misera-
ble for ever.[1]

In New England Whitefield met Puritan minister Jonathan
Edwards (1703–58), whose preaching in Northampton, Massachusetts, had sparked revival there with sermons such as "Sinners in the Hands of an Angry God." Like Whitefield and unlike the Wesley brothers, Edwards was an ardent Calvinist, but
unlike many Calvinists of that time he believed that God uses
extraordinary means to win the elect to himself. Among those
means was powerful preaching about the torments of hell and
the absolute necessity of sincere, heartfelt repentance and
faith in Jesus Christ. John and Charles Wesley, who remained
in England while their friend and colleague Whitefield
preached up and down the American coast, preferred to dwell
on God's love more than the punishments that await the unconverted in hell. Eventually differences between their Arminianism (belief in genuine free will) and Whitefield's and Edwards's Calvinism (belief in unconditional election and
irresistible grace) led to a schism between them. This difference over the background belief about God's agency and human agency in salvation has remained a rift within Evangelicalism and evangelical theology since the falling out between the
Wesleys and Whitefield.

John Wesley and Jonathan Edwards may fairly be seen as
the two great founders of Evangelicalism in the English-
speaking world. Wesley was profoundly influenced by Zinzendorf, although he rejected the German count's seeming
cult-personality status among the Moravians. Edwards was
influenced by a Pietist streak within Puritanism. His grandfather Solomon Stoddard, whose pulpit in Northampton he inherited, had preached salvation through conversion and the

---

[1]Quoted in Frank Lambert, *Inventing the "Great Awakening"* (Princeton,
NJ: Princeton University Press, 1999), 98.

absolute necessity of a life of devotion and holiness (even as he became the architect of the so-called Half-Way Covenant, which allowed unconverted children of church members to participate in the sacraments and life of the church). What makes Edwards and Wesley the founders of the evangelical movement is their tremendous influence on church and culture through their persuasive insistence on the necessity of radical conversion experience for salvation and authentic Christian existence. While both men affirmed the absolute authority of Scripture and insisted on the classical doctrines of Christian orthodoxy, they also elevated experience over doctrine as the true centerpiece of Christian existence. Each in his own way inserted "conversional piety" firmly into the mainstream of British and American religious life. Through them the message and belief that "you must be born again" became more than the peculiar distinctive of a fringe group of enthusiastic fanatics and became instead the hallmark of a major movement that inserted itself firmly and permanently within Protestant life in the English-speaking world.

4

The Puritan Roots of Evangelical Theology

Jonathan Edwards's contribution to Evangelicalism and evangelical theology is rooted in his Puritan heritage combined with his Pietist-like and revivalistic passion for conversion as a change of religious affections. Before expounding Edwards's distinctive evangelical theology and its role in shaping Evangelicalism, it will be helpful to examine Puritanism and Puritan theology. The Puritan movement began in Elizabethan England in the late sixteenth century. Scholars debate the identity of the first Puritan; that is largely a matter of definition. Puritanism broadly defined began as the English movement to purify the Church of England under Queen Elizabeth I and her appointed archbishops of Canterbury of all vestiges of "Romish" doctrine and practice. The Puritans objected to the imposition of a uniform liturgy on all churches in the English realm. They wanted to abolish the office of bishop or reduce it to an administrative role. They regarded some of the trappings of Anglican worship as more Catholic than Protestant and thus "un-Reformed." Many of them were strongly influenced by the continental Reformed tradition of Protestantism generally associated with the name of John Calvin and the city of Geneva in Switzerland. This influence was also mediated to the English Puritans by the reformer of Scotland (at that time a separate kingdom from England), John Knox (1514–72), who referred to Calvin's Geneva as the most perfect school of Christ since the days of the apostles. Knox transformed the kingdom of Scotland into a constitutional monarchy with republican aspects, with his Presbyterian Church as the national church. The Puritans in England wanted a similar thorough reform of England, but they were opposed in their efforts by Queen Elizabeth, her archbishops, and the leading theologians of Anglicanism, such as Richard Hooker (1554–1600), who wrote a multivolume defense of Anglicanism entitled *The Laws of Ecclesiastical Polity*.

The so-called Elizabethan Settlement was carefully constructed in England throughout Elizabeth's reign (1558–1603) and brought together Protestant theology (Scripture as the ultimate authority for faith and practice and justification by grace through faith alone) and some elements of Catholic polity and worship. The Puritans perceived this as unjustified compromise and argued strenuously for a thoroughly Protestant national church. They lost that part of their cause but became so powerful in England that they managed to lead a civil war in the 1640s that led to King Charles's beheading at the hands of Puritan-dominated Parliament and a brief period of Puritan rule during which Great Britain (which had included Scotland beginning in 1603) was a commonwealth (similar to a republic) under radical separatist Puritan military leader Oliver Cromwell (1599–1658). Eventually the Puritan cause was lost and both the monarchy (with the sovereign as the governor of the Church of England) and Anglican church were reestablished.

Throughout the turmoil of the first half of the seventeenth century, thousands of Puritans left England to settle in New England, where they hoped to establish a Puritan commonwealth to the glory of God, and where many of them dropped their Presbyterianism and became Congregationalists.

One of the Puritan theologians of the seventeenth century who greatly influenced the beginning and course of Evangelicalism was John Owen (1616–83), who was for a while dean of Christ Church, Oxford and served as vice-chancellor of England under Cromwell. Owen wrote numerous volumes of Puritan theology, some of which are still in print and widely read by Reformed Christians three and a half centuries later. He was a strong defender of the Congregational form of Puritanism that insisted on a "gathered church" model, in which the true, visible church consists of believers only, and the autonomy of individual congregations. He wrote against the high church Arminianism of the Church of England in the seventeenth century and argued for a strict form of Calvinist theology. He also wrote on the substitutionary atonement of Christ and the person and work of the Holy Spirit. His theological and devotional works stressed the importance of personal repentance and faith as well as of a life of holiness. Owen combined in his life and writings the distinctively Puritan blend of rigorous Reformed-Calvinistic doctrine (unconditional election and irresistible grace) and strict spirituality revolving around repentance, prayer and devotional exercises, Bible reading and study, and other Protestant spiritual disciplines. Owen and other seventeenth-century Puritan divines (minister-theologians) displayed a decidedly pietistic attitude toward Christian life before the Pietist movement began in Europe, but they did not highlight the emotional and decisionistic aspects of authentic Christian experience as much as later Pietists. For them, salvation was a process that began at the moment Christ died on the cross for the sins of all the elect (thus the title of Owens's best-known book, *The Death of Death in the Death of Christ*); continued through infant baptism (children are born into the "covenant people of God") and childhood Christian nurture within the home and church; and included repentance, faith, confession of doctrinal belief, and a daily life of devotion and discipleship. Revivalism was not envisaged by the Puritans before Jonathan Edwards, but they did emphasize the absolute necessity of true Christianity as *visible Christianity* showing forth in "signs of grace," including ability to express one's struggle from preparation for personal faith through repentance and conversion into assurance of salvation and solid church membership and good citizenship. Of course, they stressed that all of this is completely dependent upon the supernatural grace of God and is for the glory of God and not the exaltation of the individual.

The Puritan vision of authentic Christianity was brought to the New England colonies of Massachusetts and Connecticut by ministers such as Thomas Hooker (1586–1647), who converted from Anglicanism to Puritanism of the Congregational variety while a student at Cambridge University. Under persecution by the crown and state church for his noncomformity (e.g., refusing to use the *Book of Common Prayer* in worship), to find religious freedom Hooker fled first to Holland and then to Cambridge, Massachusetts, where he pastored a Puritan congregation. In 1636 he led his entire congregation into the wilderness to found the city of Hartford and establish the commonwealth of Connecticut. Hooker wrote an influential volume on Congregational polity and social theory entitled *Survey of the Summe of Church Discipline* (1648) and taught his own unique form of "federal theology," which was the distinctively Puritan form of Reformed covenant theology. According to Hooker's federal theology God deals with humanity through covenants (social-spiritual contracts), and so long as human persons keep their side of the bargain God is obligated (by his promise) to bless them with spiritual and material blessings.

One can know that one is part of God's elect (predestined) people and destined for heaven by examining one's own covenant-keeping in inward attitudes and outward disciplines. This is also how the gathered church discerns which of all the inhabitants of a city or colony are fit for full church membership including participation in the sacrament of the Lord's Supper.

Throughout the seventeenth century the original zeal of Puritanism in both England and the New England colonies cooled considerably. By the turn of the new century (1701) in most Puritan churches it was difficult to tell which church attenders were true believers and which were mere "professors" of Christian religion. The gathered churches of New England were becoming mixed assemblies as children and grandchildren of the Puritan diaspora of the 1630s and 1640s grew up within the congregations and simply learned how to play their roles without ever experiencing the stages of conversion or giving testimony of radical repentance or showing signs of grace in their lives. Arminian theology—once the sworn enemy of the Calvinist Puritans—was bleeding out of the congregations of the Church of England and into the Presbyterian and Congregational churches of the Puritans as well as into their colleges for ministerial training. The elders of Puritanism in New England, such as Jonathan Edwards's grandfather Solomon Stoddard (1643–1729), created compromises in order to keep the unconverted children of Puritans active within the Puritan congregations. The so-called Half-Way Covenant, of which Stoddard was a main architect, allowed unconverted but baptized children of Puritan church members to partake of the Lord's Supper with the hope that it would serve as a "converting influence" in their lives and the lives of their children. Eventually their children were baptized and allowed to grow up within the church without ever being required to recount their experiences of repentance and coming to know Christ as redeemer and Lord.

By 1730 New England was ripe for spiritual and theological

renewal. The majority of its inhabitants participated in church worship and sacraments merely because they had been born "in the covenant" and had never chosen to opt out of it. (Church attendance was required in most places, but passionate participation in the life of the church was not.) The line of demarcation between nominal Christianity and authentic Christianity that had been so fiercely identified and defended by the first Puritans was blurred at best. Jonathan Edwards came from a long line of Puritans and was by all accounts a child prodigy with a strong interest in the life of the mind well before he entered Yale College in 1716. He became his grandfather's associate pastor at the Congregational church in Northampton, Massachusetts, in 1724 and then succeeded him as pastor in 1729. He was intensely interested in the new philosophy emanating from Europe and Great Britain that later came to be known as Enlightenment science and philosophy, and he was especially influenced by some of the ideas of the philosopher John Locke. His greatest passion, however, was biblical study and exposition. While he is best known for his sermon "Sinners in the Hands of an Angry God," Edwards also wrote calm, well-reasoned treatises on philosophy, biblical themes, science, theology, and religious experience. His sermons tended to be strongly doctrinal, with emphasis upon the necessity of repentance to avoid the wrath of God. His theological underpinnings were strongly Calvinistic with the flavoring of federal theology. His two overriding themes were the glory of God and human dependence upon God and God's grace for everything. He attributed all that happens to the sovereign providence of God and affirmed God's justice in condemning some portion of humanity to hell by his own free, sovereign good pleasure.

Throughout the 1730s Edwards was quietly, persistently preparing his Northampton congregation and his entire network of like-minded Puritan ministers for a spiritual renewal. There had been something like revivals before, but by and large they had been local and with little lasting effect. Many Puritans were wary of emotional appeals for individual decision for Christ, preferring instead a quiet preparation of souls for repentance and faith within the normal structures of Word and sacrament within the local churches. During the 1730s New England Puritans, including Edwards and his congregation, heard of a new phenomenon taking place primarily within the Church of England in London and other English cities. George Whitefield's fame as a stirring preacher, who held crowds spellbound out of doors and to whose sermons hundreds and even thousands responded by becoming "born again," preceded his arrival in Philadelphia in 1739. When Whitefield arrived in New England, he and Edwards almost immediately bonded in friendship and ministry. Edwards's own congregation had begun to experience an "awakening" in 1734 with people crying out during the minister's sermons and sometimes falling to the ground speechless in sorrow for their sins and fear of hell. Many were profoundly converted and, according to Edwards, the spiritual atmosphere of the entire town was uplifted.

In 1737 he wrote a defense of the Northampton revival entitled *A Faithful Narrative of the Surprising Work of God in the Conversion of Many Hundred Souls in Northampton, and the Neighboring Towns and Villages.* Leading Presbyterian and Congregational ministers and theologians were harshly critical of the revivals that preceded Whitefield's arrival, and they ridiculed him and those who swarmed to his "imported Divinity" once he arrived. Nevertheless, the ground was prepared for the Great Awakening, and for about fifteen years wave after wave of highly emotional responses to preaching by itinerant ministers swept the New England and middle colonies. The centerpiece of all the commotion was the experience of the "new birth." The revivalists—led primarily by Edwards and Whitefield— proclaimed an immediate change of heart, soul, and mind brought about by the Spirit of God whenever a person truly repented and trusted in Jesus Christ alone for salvation. Edwards brought his mind to bear on the controversy over the revivals, which were being labeled "enthusiasm" (which meant roughly what "fanaticism" means today) in several essays and treatises. Most notably he examined the criteria by which false religious affections could be distinguished from true religious affections in *A Treatise Concerning Religious Affections* (1746).

What did Edwards contribute to the evangelical movement and its theology? Without any doubt his main contribution was and remains his incisive examination of the nature of human persons and how they are ruled by *affections* more than by reason or free will. The affections are roughly what is meant by "heart" in popular evangelical preaching and teaching. According to Edwards, the reason and will are both governed by an inner core of personality that he labeled affections. One is what one loves, and salvation is an act of God upon the affections. Without reducing authentic religion (Christianity) to affections, Edwards more closely identified them than almost anyone before him: "From hence it clearly and certainly appears, that great part of true religion consists in the affections. For love is not only one of the affections, but it is the first and chief of the affections, and the fountain of all the affections."[1] Most theologians of Edwards's day emphasized either the will or the mind as the chief "seat" of human actions and thus appealed to one or both for religious renewal. Either persons were urged to study, understand, and confess true doctrine, or they were exhorted to exercise their wills toward higher moral endeavor. Many distrusted emotions and affections. Jonathan Edwards did not necessarily trust emotions and affections, but

---

[1]Jonathan Edwards, "Religious Affections," in *Jonathan Edwards: Representative Selections,* ed. Clarence H. Faust and Thomas H. Johnson, rev. ed. (New York: Hill & Wang, 1962), 220.

he did regard them as the seat of true religion, including authentic Christianity. A person who is truly converted to Christ will have "benevolence for being" placed in him or her by the grace and mercy of God and will display that in acts of loving-kindness. Edwards had little use for excessive displays of emotion, although he did not think they were always necessarily evil or contrary to true Christian faith; he simply preferred the manifestation of love. Both he and Whitefield believed that this inward change of affections could take place only by the power of God's Spirit through a new birth and that such an experience would always be a work of sovereign grace (God's free choice, predestination) that appeared to be freely chosen by the repentant sinner in response to God's Word proclaimed.

The Great Awakening transformed the culture of the New World, which was imbued with a profound religious sensitivity. Churches throughout the colonies took sides either for or against Whitefield and the revivals. New churches sprang up wherever the established churches opposed the revivals; even though the revival fires eventually burned lower, revivalism remained a permanent feature of life in the North American colonies and the United States of America. Evangelicalism as a movement was born in the 1730s and 1740s Great Awakening.

5

The Wesleyan Roots of Evangelical Theology

John Wesley picked up in England where Whitefield left off when he boarded a ship for the colonies in 1739. Whitefield and John and Charles Wesley had become close friends while students at Oxford University where they formed the core of the Holy Club—a student conventicle for practicing spiritual disciplines. John Wesley became a priest of the Church of England as did Whitefield, but while Whitefield became an itinerant preacher to coal miners and Londoners in the parks, Wesley became a parish priest and short-term missionary to the colony of Georgia. Eventually Wesley experienced a much-needed spiritual awakening in a Moravian meeting, where someone was reading Luther's Introduction to his *Commentary on Paul's Epistle to the Romans*. He felt his heart "strangely warmed" and received assurance of his salvation. Some Wesley scholars have argued that this was Wesley's new birth experience while others have argued that he was already born again and this was simply an assurance of that. In any case, Wesley considered this a turning point in his spiritual life, and afterwards he was more willing to take Whitefield's open-air preaching style to those who would not or could not enter church buildings to hear the gospel. With his brother Charles writing the songs and leading the singing, John traveled around England preaching the love of God for all people and everyone's need of repentance in order to receive the grace and mercy of God unto salvation. While Wesley never repudiated infant baptism as a sacrament, he definitely believed and preached that every person—baptized or not—needs a conversion and new birth by repentance and faith. This is expressed in numerous of Wesley's sermons, such as "Scriptural Christianity" and "Justification by Faith." For Wesley, true "scriptural Christianity" begins in a person with the experience of being "born anew" by the Spirit of God. Of course, he did not deny the efficacy of the sacrament of infant baptism, but he did deny that it alone establishes a person's right relationship with God. For Wesley, authentic Christianity is *experiential Christianity* and must be freely chosen; it can never be inherited or the product of an effort to "turn over a new leaf." Nor can it be caused by a sacrament of the church alone.

By experiential (or "experimental") Christianity Wesley did not mean salvation by emotions or willpower ("enthusiasm"). He believed that only God can save a person and that if a person is saved it is entirely due to God's grace, but people must respond to God's grace and to the gospel with a free decision of repentance and faith. He was theologically Arminian rather than Calvinist. This led to a falling out with his friend Whitefield, who agreed that people must decide for Christ in order to be saved, but also believed that such decisions are always foreordained by God. Wesley did not agree; he believed that free decisions are foreknown but not foreordained. Wesley and Whitefield agreed entirely, however, on the crucial dimension of revivalism: appeal to persons to make decisions for Christ through repenting of their sins and trusting in Christ alone for forgiveness and inward renewal. Wesley wrote of his response to those who trusted in their baptism for full salvation:

> I tell a sinner, "You must be born again." "No," say you, "He was born again in baptism. Therefore he cannot be born again now." Alas! What trifling is this? What if he was then a child of God? He is now manifestly a "child of the devil"? . . . Therefore do not play upon words. He must go through an entire change of heart [without which] if either he or you die . . . your baptism will be so far from profiting you that it will greatly increase your damnation.[1]

Wesley recognized two conditions for receiving this "entire change of heart"—true repentance and true belief in Jesus Christ as God's Son and one's own only Savior. *True* is meant to distinguish these conditions from mere mental sorrow and intellectual belief. For Wesley, as for Whitefield, genuine repentance and genuine faith in Jesus Christ necessarily involve the whole person and must be reflected in a change of life that is visible to others. Wesley made absolutely clear in his theological writings that this change from the old life to a new life is a work of God and that apart from God's prevenient (calling and assisting) grace no person could ever exercise true repentance or true faith and be saved.

One aspect of Wesley's theology that gained partial acceptance among evangelicals but was rejected by others is "Christian perfection"—his distinctive idea of sanctification. In spite of its rejection by more Reformed evangelicals including Whitefield and even the Pietist leader Zinzendorf, Wesley's

---

[1]Quoted in Thomas C. Oden, *John Wesley's Scriptural Christianity* (Grand Rapids: Zondervan, 1994), 302.

teaching that Christians could attain eradication of the sinful
impulses and all presumptuous sinning entered into the evangelical movement and left a profound impression there. Even
evangelical persons and groups that believe sanctification will
always remain a process until death (the traditional Reformed
view) have often absorbed some degree of Wesley's perfectionism, and it has appeared in revivalists, theologians, and sub-
movements of Evangelicalism that are not specifically Wesleyan (e.g., Charles Finney and later the Keswick movement).
In a little book entitled *A Plain Account of Christian Perfection*
Wesley spelled out his notion of entire sanctification. According to him, it is possible for Christians, by the power of the Holy
Spirit appropriated by faith, to reach a state of inner transformation where the struggle against the "world, flesh, and devil"
cease and conscious, willful, presumptuous sinning never
again disrupts the Christian's relationship with God or others.
Wesley made abundantly clear in the little book that he did not
mean such entirely sanctified persons would rise above all flaw
or fault, and he affirmed that they would continue to commit
sins of omission out of ignorance or even goodwill (e.g., trusting people too much). While Wesley did not claim to have
reached such a stage in his Christian life, he did offer accounts
of others who had reached it. He did not consider entire sanctification abnormal or a mark of particular saintliness. Rather,
he treated it as the normal Christian experience for all who
seek and receive it by faith. Later Wesleyans sometimes added
to Wesley's doctrine of sanctification an initiation experience
often called the "second blessing," which they believed would
catapult persons wholly submissive to God's will and power into
a sin-free existence. Many nineteenth-century revivals inspired
by Wesley's followers featured "mourners' benches" at the
front of the sanctuary or revival tent, where seekers after entire
sanctification could "tarry" in prayer for the experience. Often
such "tarrying meetings" after revival sermons lasted for hours

and were marked by great emotion. What Wesley would have thought about this Holiness movement that erupted a few decades after his death along the margins of his Methodist movement is unknown and a favorite subject of speculation among Wesley scholars.

6

The Crucible of Modern Evangelical Theology in the Great Awakenings

Evangelicalism and evangelical theology were born in the eighteenth-century Great Awakening in England and North America. They had a gestation period if not a preexistence in continental Pietism. Jonathan Edwards and John Wesley are the two fathers of evangelical Christianity, which had numerous ancestors (e.g., the Anabaptists and Puritans) and aunts and uncles (e.g., Quakers, Separatists, Baptists, Scottish Holy Fairs, the Jansenists). Something quite new appeared out of the Great Awakening and Edwards's and Wesley's sermons and essays—a mass movement, a subculture of experiential Christianity solidly rooted in Protestant orthodoxy.

Edwards and Wesley also bequeathed to Evangelicalism and evangelical theology a legacy of tension between two competing paradigms of Protestant orthodoxy—Reformed (Calvinist) theology and free-will theism (Arminianism). Edwards, together with his Puritan forebears and followers, believed that God's sovereignty is absolute and unconditioned by humans' decisions and actions except insofar as they are foreordained by God himself. Furthermore, Edwards taught that human beings are born totally depraved and utterly dependent on God's sovereign grace, mercy, and regenerating power for their salvation (should they be so fortunate as to be among the elect). When Edwards preached his famous revival sermon "Sinners in the Hands of an Angry God," he did not intend his listeners to conclude that their salvation from God's wrath against sin depended on their own free choices and actions. Instead, he inculcated in his listeners the belief that, though they must repent and believe in order to be saved from God's wrath and eternal torment in hell, their eternal destinies really depended entirely upon God's free decision of election and regeneration; their decisions to repent and believe would be sovereign works of God in them. God would create the new affections and cause them to be "born again," and only then would they experience affection for God and benevolence for all beings.

Wesley, on the other hand, preached and wrote about the free will of human beings without denying total depravity (or what he preferred to call "deprivation") and divine sovereignty. He believed that God gives to each person some measure of "prevenient grace" that enables him or her to make a free decision in response to the gospel call to repent and believe. Whereas Edwards emphasized the glory and majesty of God and the inability and dependence of humanity, Wesley emphasized the love of God and human persons' ability to respond to God on the basis of God's gift of assisting grace. These two streams of thought about salvation entered into Evangelicalism and have been present ever since. They have made evangelical theology an unstable compound always about to explode into internecine rivalry, if not warfare.

The revivalist impulse that gave birth to modern Evangelicalism during the Great Awakening became part of the fabric of American society and especially of its religious life. Unfortunately, many, if not most, of the revivals and revivalists after that did not live up to the high standards set by Edwards, Whitefield, and John and Charles Wesley. Evangelicals have always looked back upon them and their Great Awakening as the "Golden Age" of evangelical life. And yet there have been numerous effective revivals since then that have given great impetus to evangelical growth and stimulated evangelical thought about the gospel, salvation, the church, and Christian living.

The so-called Second Great Awakening was a diffuse collection of revivals in New England and along the North American frontier during the last decade of the eighteenth century and first three decades of the nineteenth century. Like the original Great Awakening, the Second Great Awakening is much debated by historians: When did it begin? What was it exactly? When did it end?[1] Whatever its exact nature and parameters may have been, the Second Great Awakening profoundly affected the religious landscape of the new United States of America and through missionary endeavors sparked by it influenced much of the world. By some accounts it began in 1795 at Yale College in Connecticut under the leadership of its president, Timothy Dwight, Jonathan Edwards's grandson. Dwight preached passionately against what he perceived to be increasing infidelity among Yale's students and engaged in vigorous classroom defenses of the authority of the Bible and supernatural work of God in salvation. A revival of Christianity broke out among the students with numerous remarkable conver-

---

[1]For an example of scholarly debate about the nature of the first, original Great Awakening, see Frank Lambert, *Inventing the "Great Awakening"* (Princeton, NJ: Princeton University Press, 1999).

sions; soon the awakening was spreading to other campuses and cities in New England. One of Dwight's best students, Lyman Beecher, carried the revival to cities in New England and then to the frontier towns and cities.

At about the same time, in Kentucky a revival began that was marked by protracted camp meetings attended by thousands of men and women and their families living on the frontier. The largest, at Cane Ridge in 1801, was led by Barton Stone, who went on later to found one of the first American-born Christian denominations, the Christian Churches. The Cane Ridge camp meeting revival and others like it witnessed amazing displays of fervent preaching and emotional responses. Hundreds and perhaps thousands of churches were started out of the camp meetings, and several denominations were born. Both the New England and frontier revivals focused on the necessity of personal, free decisions of repentance and acceptance of Christ for the salvation experience of being "born again."

Perhaps the single most influential person associated with the Second Great Awakening was the evangelist Charles G. Finney (1792–1875), who left an indelible mark upon nineteenth-century Christianity in North America. Some historians have called him the first true American evangelist. He certainly established a pattern for most later independent evangelists and revivalists. He organized highly efficient and productive mass evangelistic campaigns on the assumption that revivals of religion are humanly contrived and are not sovereign works of God's grace. Finney was an attorney by profession, but he experienced a radical conversion on October 10, 1821, in Adams, New York, after which he left his law practice and entered the Presbyterian ministry. He eventually switched to Congregationalism, as it allowed greater freedom for his own style of entrepreneurial evangelism. Finney met with great success and public acclaim as he preached revivals from town to town and city to city throughout New York and New England and Great Britain. His methods were based on business; he did not believe in waiting for God's Spirit to "move," but instead manipulated revivals with prerevival publicity and citywide ministerial cooperation and preparation. His preaching focused on God's moral government of humanity and humanity's rebelliousness against God's moral government and need and ability to repent and return to obedience to God's moral demands. His *Lectures on Revivals of Religion* (1835) laid out a program for initiating revivals and argued that revivals automatically occur when churches plan for them in the right ways, including prayer and social justice. Finney believed and taught that one of the greatest hindrances to revivals is social injustice, including slavery and denial of equality to women.

Finney's theology was strongly Arminian, if not semi-Pelagian. That is, unlike Edwards and Whitefield before him, he believed that humans have a natural ability from God to decide to repent, trust in Christ, and obey God's moral law. He denied unconditional election and irresistible grace and radically reinterpreted divine sovereignty and providence. His was a gospel message and program for Christian renewal that fit with the individualistic and activist temper of the times. Thousands of people "accepted Christ," often with great emotion, in Finney's revival meetings, which often lasted for weeks in the same city. Eventually Finney settled in Oberlin, Ohio, and became professor of theology and then president of Oberlin College, where he led the students and faculty in acts of civil disobedience against slavery and admitted women students to ministerial courses of study.

The Second Great Awakening, including Finney's revivalism, left an impact on evangelical Christianity that lasts into the twenty-first century. Without denying the "unpredictable sovereignty of God's grace," these revivalists, ministers, and theologians elevated human means of bringing about individual and mass conversions and tended to regard Christian endeavors from evangelism to church planting to social reform as activities of humans inspired and empowered by God's Spirit. The older Puritan ideas of total depravity and human dependence upon God's initiative were demoted and often even ignored. Pragmatic criteria of success replaced more traditional and stringent tests of works of God and manifestations of God's kingdom. Many of these revivals—including Finney's—were transdenominational, leading to a lessening of denominational identities and loyalties. By and large, basic Protestant orthodoxy was assumed and, when necessary, defended by the Second Great Awakening revivalists; those on the margins of the renewal were pushed out when they espoused heterodox or heretical views. The so-called Burnt-Over District of western New York witnessed the rise of numerous homegrown sects and cults toward the end of the Second Great Awakening. Nevertheless, the Evangelicalism of the early nineteenth-century revivals was a form of experiential Christianity that placed premium value on human cooperation with divine grace and the Holy Spirit in initiating and establishing works of God. One example was Finney's innovation called the "anxious bench," where people who felt first stirrings of God's work in their lives calling them to Christ sat during his preaching. Finney and later imitators would direct arguments toward them, enticing them with reason as well as with traditional exhortation from the Bible to believe the gospel, repent, and embrace Christ as Savior and Lord.

Later evangelical revivalists and evangelists who influenced the course of Evangelicalism and its theology included Dwight Lyman Moody (1837–99), Billy Sunday (1862–1935), Aimee Semple McPherson (1890–1944), and Billy Graham (b. 1918). All followed in the footsteps of Charles Finney, and each, in his or her own way, appealed to emotion and will in order to bring listeners to "personal decisions for Christ" so that they were converted. All assumed that people in their multidenominational audiences were not already authentic Christians merely because they were born in the United States or baptized as infants into a Christian church. All believed in and preached a basic Protestant orthodoxy that included the supreme authority of the Bible, a supernatural life and worldview, a personal and transcendent God who is in charge of nature and history, and Jesus Christ as God, Lord, and Savior. Each one led a new Great Awakening during his or her own time, and out of their revivalist campaigns arose new churches and denominations determined to restore authentic, primitive Christianity as it was in the New Testament in the days of the apostles. Each of them assumed an "evangelical synergism" in which God initiates the event of salvation through the proclaimed Word and human hearers complete it through making the appropriate response freely, often with tears and confessions of sin.

Through the revivalist tradition Evangelicalism became what some historians have called "America's folk religion."[2] That is, it became a transdenominational, grassroots movement including millions of ordinary people with differing lifestyles and class identities who embraced a common stock of beliefs that were held together by two basic themes: the Bible as God's infallible, authoritative Word and salvation through a personal experience of conversion to Christ followed by a personal relationship with Jesus Christ in everyday life. The preaching of evangelical revivalists was and is always based on biblical passages, and appeal is to the authority of the Bible as God's written Word. Evangelicals have acknowledged the Bible as a unique book supernaturally inspired by God, and they have loved to read and study it. They have also believed that authentic Christianity begins with a personal "crisis experience"

---

[2]See Randall Balmer, *Mine Eyes Have Seen the Glory: A Journey Through America's Evangelical Subculture* (New York: Oxford University Press, 1989).

that involves a decision to repent and trust in Christ alone for salvation (conversion). This "folk religion" has developed its own common stock of stories, songs, customs, habits, and forms of life that cross many denominational boundaries. For many evangelicals, being evangelical is as important as or more important than being Methodist, Baptist, Presbyterian, or any other denomination.

Revivalists were primarily concerned about the prevalence of what some of them called "dead orthodoxy" among church members. They were also concerned, of course, about the masses of people who had no knowledge of the gospel or had left the churches and had no particular connection with organized Christianity. Their evangelical response to nominal Christianity and modern paganism was, "Repent and be born again." Their vision of authentic Christianity and fulfilled humanity was and is "conversional piety"—a personal relationship with God through Jesus Christ that begins with and is maintained by repentance of sin and personal, heartfelt trust in Jesus Christ and his death on the cross for sins. Revivalists usually felt no special calling to defend Protestant orthodoxy; they assumed it and added the dimension of experiential Christianity. Another group of nineteenth-century evangelicals, however, who came to be called fundamentalists, believed that the greatest threat to authentic Christianity and fulfilled humanity ("man fully alive") was not dead orthodoxy but paganism (i.e., life lived apart from Christian commitment) or modern secularism manifested in philosophical and theological skepticism. These evangelicals often sympathized and cooperated with some revivalists, but their special "calling" was to be apostles to those adversely affected by the Enlightenment's acids of modernity and especially to Christian denominations and churches that were falling under secularism's influence and creating a new brand of Christian theology called "liberal theology." Whereas revivalists and their followers elevated *orthopathy*—right affections—as the most important test of authentic Christianity, fundamentalists elevated *orthodoxy*—right beliefs—as the most important test of authentic Christianity. To be sure, both groups of evangelicals valued *orthopraxy*—right behavior—as a test of authentic Christianity, but neither of them considered it ultimate in guiding and determining authentic Christianity. Liberal theology tended to specialize in orthopraxy—especially in matters of social reform.

7

Old Princeton Theology and Evangelical Theology

The Enlightenment of the eighteenth century was a cultural revolution in Europe, Great Britain, and North America that was summed up, according to German philosopher Immanuel Kant, in the phrase *sapere aude!*—"think for yourself." It was a revolt against the stifling authorities of tradition and dogmatic religion and a search for truth through autonomous human reason without any appeal to special revelation, faith, or tradition. It had its philosophical and scientific manifestations, and in religion it gave rise to three main movements: deism, unitarianism, and liberal Protestantism. All three sought to reform Protestant Christianity along Enlightenment lines by appealing to common reason, public evidence, natural religion and theology, and universal human spiritual experience. Enlightenment thinkers sought to undermine the absolute authority of theological tradition and the Bible by demonstrating inconsistencies, errors, discrepancies between texts and translations, and other flaws. Not all Enlightenment thinkers were anti-Christian, but most tended to believe it good and necessary to question traditional Christian beliefs. Pietists and revivalists thought that the best response to dead orthodoxy and modern paganism was also the best response to Enlightenment secularism and skepticism: proclamation of the gospel of Jesus Christ and appeal to people to repent and trust in Christ alone for salvation. Had not John Calvin himself argued that belief in the Bible as God's Word is by the "internal testimony of the Holy Spirit" and not by arguments and evidences? Fundamentalists, however, believed that the best response to the "acids of modernity" was tearing down "proud arguments" and militantly exposing them as errors, as well as strong reaffirmation of traditional, orthodox beliefs.

The prehistory of fundamentalism as an antimodernist and antiliberal evangelical movement begins with the so-called Princeton School of theology, best exemplified by five great Presbyterian theologians who taught at Princeton Theological Seminary in the nineteenth and early twentieth centuries: Archibald Alexander (1772–1851), Charles Hodge (1797–1878), Archibald Alexander Hodge (1823–86), Benjamin Breckenridge Warfield (1851–1921), and John Gresham Machen (1881–1937). Many evangelical Christians, especially evangelical theologians, look back to these Reformed exponents of Protestant orthodoxy as the true movers and shakers of evangelical theology, while admitting that Evangelicalism's folk religion is shaped more by revivalism.[1] J. Gresham Machen is often treated as the first and perhaps the greatest "true fundamentalist theologian" by historians of American Christianity, but he stood in a direct line of theological influence from

---

[1]See for example David Wells, *No Place for Truth: Whatever Happened to Evangelical Theology?* (Grand Rapids: Wm. B. Eerdmans, 1993) and "The Stout and Persistent 'Theology' of Charles Hodge," *Christianity Today* 18, no. 23 (August 30, 1974): 10-15.

Alexander through the Hodges (father and son) and Warfield (Machen's mentor). The Princeton School of theology and early fundamentalism (at its best) believed that authentic Christianity's enduring essence is orthodox doctrine—theological correctness—and attempted to systematize and defend it against the rising tides of Enlightenment skepticism and liberal Protestantism. In the process they sometimes forged uneasy alliances with revivalists, but by and large they did not consider Second Great Awakening revivalism and the Evangelicalism that stemmed from it very helpful. Nevertheless, they had a common enemy—skepticism about the truth claims of the gospel—and so they sometimes cooperated in spite of profound differences of style and substance.

Charles Hodge taught theology to more than two thousand students at Princeton Theological Seminary during his fifty-six-year tenure (1822–78). Without any doubt he was the most influential conservative Protestant theologian of nineteenth-century America. Although Hodge and Finney were very different, the comparison between them is irresistible. Hodge placed his stamp upon conservative evangelical theology just as Finney placed his stamp upon revivalistic Evangelicalism and the evangelical theology that has arisen within evangelical folk religion. They are probably the two most influential nineteenth-century evangelicals, and yet they were in many ways as different as night and day. Hodge was an ardent Calvinist steeped in Protestant scholasticism—the post-Reformation tendency to use rigorous logical methods to systematize the truths of divine revelation in Scripture. He was a powerful polemicist who argued vehemently against any and all deviations from traditional, orthodox Protestant belief among Christians. He was a social conservative who defended slavery and traditional gender roles in family and church. Just as Finney's *Lectures on Revivals of Religion* and *Lectures on Systematic Theology* influenced evangelicals inclined toward revivalism, Hodge's three-volume *Systematic Theology* (1872–73) profoundly influenced evangelicals inclined toward fundamentalism.

Hodge believed that the best way to confront and counter the deleterious effects of the Enlightenment upon Christianty was to use its own methods in defense of the truth of Christianity. This he sought to do without capitulation or compromise by defining Christian theology as a science. Of course, he was not the first to regard theology as a "science" in the sense of "wisdom" or "disciplined study," but Hodge opened his systematic theology by describing it as an inductive science of facts similar to the natural sciences: "We find in nature the facts which the chemist or the mechanical philosopher has to examine, and from them to ascertain the laws by which they are determined. So the Bible contains the truths which the theologian has to collect, authenticate, arrange, and exhibit in their internal relation to each other."[2] Throughout his systematic theology Hodge attempted to demonstrate that theology is scientific in the modern sense and not at all superstitious or obscurantist. Just as the natural scientist observes natural phenomena and organizes its data and deduces principles from it, so the theological scientist observes divine revelation in Scripture and organizes its truths into a coherent whole that, as a whole, provides a better explanation of the universe and human life than any competing philosophy or theology.

Thus, Hodge tended to treat the Bible as a presystematized systematic theology and systematic theology as a comprehensive, rationally coherent worldview. Some critics have labeled this approach to theology the "evangelical Enlightenment" because it so closely parallels the general attitude of the Enlightenment toward knowledge. The particular branch of the Enlightenment being used to understand Hodge in this case is

[2]Charles Hodge, *Systematic Theology,* vol. 1 (Grand Rapids: Wm. B. Eerdmans, 1973), 1.

Scottish common sense realism, which argued against David Hume's skepticism that reasonable people are allowed to make certain assumptions about the objective reality of nature outside the mind and about our human mind and senses and their ability to grasp that reality. Hodge seemed to believe that if he could present conservative Reformed Protestant theology as a rationally coherent system of divinely revealed facts, a system that explains human existence better than any competing account, the tide of modern skepticism could be resisted. This approach to theology was taken up by later evangelical theologians and made the basis of many truth claims about its superiority to secular and liberal systems of thought.

Another area of Hodge's theology that profoundly influenced later fundamentalism and conservative evangelical theology is his doctrine of Scripture. Hodge stood in a tradition that highly valued Scripture as God's Word written and as authoritative above traditions. He noticed a trend toward redefining Scripture's authority within the churches being affected by Enlightenment modernism, and he wanted to guard and protect the Bible from its critics both inside and outside the church. He developed a doctrine of Scripture that he believed would do that—the doctrine of the Bible's verbal, plenary inspiration and infallibility. While denying that Scripture (the canon of sixty-six books that compose the Protestant Bible) was written under any mechanical compulsion, Hodge argued that the supernatural process of communication known as "inspiration" extended from God through the human authors to the very words, with the result that what they wrote were the very words of God and thus infallible:

> On this subject the common doctrine of the Church is, and ever has been, that inspiration was an influence of the Holy Spirit on the minds of certain select men, which rendered them the organs of God for the infallible com-

munication of his mind and will. They were in such a sense the organs of God, that what they said God said.[3]

Hodge argued that since God controls human beings in salvation without robbing them of their personalities, God can and did control the human authors of Scripture, so that they wrote what he wanted them to write, without in any way detracting from their personal involvement in the process. The Bible, then, is God's oracle to humanity. Even if there are minor inconsistencies and discrepancies in it, Hodge averred, they are not sufficient to detract from its supernatural origin and authority. For the Princeton theologian, only this account of Scripture upholds its authority; any other one (mystical, intuitionist, naturalistic) undermines its authority and thereby undermines Christian truth.

A later Princeton theologian, even closer to fundamentalism than Hodge, attempted to nail down even more firmly this high doctrine of Scripture in the face of mounting skepticism about the Bible's reliability and compatibility with modern knowledge. Benjamin Breckenridge Warfield taught systematic theology at Princeton beginning in 1887. During his tenure at the Presbyterian seminary, so-called modernism or theological liberalism began to be felt on its faculty, and Warfield fought against it with all his might. Like Hodge, whom he greatly admired, he was an ardent Calvinist and had little sympathy for the revivalist movement among evangelicals. Also like Hodge, he considered true evangelical Christianity to be synonymous with confessional Protestant orthodoxy, which he thought was entirely dependent upon a view of Scripture as verbally inspired and inerrant. Warfield's legacy to fundamentalism and conservative evangelical theology is largely in his volume *Revelation and Inspiration,* which contains several essays on subjects related to the Bible and in which the Princeton theologian ar-

---

[3]Ibid., 154.

gued that strict inerrancy of Scripture is necessary to its authority. Warfield never tired of arguing that any demonstrable error in the Bible would necessarily mean that it is not trustworthy as God's authoritative Word and that Christianity would in that case rest on very shaky ground.

The Princeton theologian was locked in debate with the beginnings of influential higher criticism of the Bible in his own denomination and the wider Protestant world. Some liberal theologians such as Washington Gladden and biblical scholars such as Charles Briggs were calling for fairly radical revisions of Christian doctrines, including the doctrine of Scripture, in the light of modern knowledge. Among other things, the reconstructionists claimed that belief in the Bible's supernatural, plenary, verbal inspiration and infallibility or inerrancy was no longer possible due to inconsistencies within Scripture itself and between scriptural texts and known facts of history and cosmology. Warfield was incensed by such claims and argued that they were based on shaky evidence and conflicted not only with secondary Christian beliefs but with Christianity's very foundations. Unlike certain later fundamentalist theologians, he did not claim that Christianity itself, let alone the gospel of Jesus Christ, rests necessarily on the doctrine of plenary, verbal inspiration; but he did claim that denial of it inevitably undermines other, if not all, fundamental Christian beliefs. He extended this reasoning to Scripture's inerrancy, which he saw as a logical deduction from its supernatural inspiration as "God's oracles." If Scripture contains errors in any subject, he asked, how is it to be trusted even in matters pertaining to salvation?

Because of this conflict with the skeptics, Warfield defined the Christian doctrine of Scripture more precisely than most Protestant theologians before him:

> The Church, then, has held from the beginning that the Bible is the Word of God in such a sense that its words,

though written by men and bearing indelibly impressed upon them the marks of their human origin, were written, nevertheless, under such an influence of the Holy Ghost as to be also the words of God, the adequate expression of His mind and will. It has always recognized that this conception of co-authorship implies that the Spirit's superintendence extends to the choice of the words by the human authors (verbal inspiration), and preserves its product from everything inconsistent with a divine authorship—thus securing, among other things, that entire truthfulness which is everywhere presupposed in and asserted for Scripture by the Biblical writers (inerrancy).[4]

Warfield argued that this definition of the doctrine of Scripture by no means implies divine dictation, although some critics have had great difficulty distinguishing the two. The Princeton theologian also argued that this is the Christian doctrine of Scripture because it is the doctrine held by the biblical writers themselves, and that to question it is to question the credibility of the Bible itself.[5]

Thus, Warfield sought to stave off the attacks on traditional Christianity by skeptics and revisionists by affirming and defending the Bible's absoluteness—including detailed, technical inerrancy—as God's oracles. The Bible contains "difficulties" and these may appear to be minor errors, he admitted, but these were becoming fewer as historical studies and archeology confirmed more and more of the biblical record; those difficulties (e.g., discrepancies, apparent contradictions) that remain are so minor as to represent no real problem for

---

[4]Benjamin Breckinridge Warfield, *The Inspiration and Authority of the Bible* (Philadelphia: Presbyterian & Reformed Publishing Co., 1948), 173.

[5]Ibid., 175.

believing in Scripture's trustworthiness. He compared them to the specks of sandstone detected here and there in the marble of the Parthenon: "They do not for the most part require explaining away, but only to be fairly understood in order to avoid them. They constitute no real strain upon faith, but when approached in a candid spirit one is left continually marveling at the excessive fewness of those which do not, like ghosts, melt away from vision as soon as faced."[6] In Warfield's hands, then, the Bible became an impregnable fortress of faith providing absolute certainty beyond reasonable doubt about all matters crucial to salvation. For if it is God's infallible oracle, as it claims to be and as it proves itself to be, it serves as a proper foundation for the edifice of Christian belief in an often hostile, increasingly secular and skeptical world, as well as in an increasingly apostate church.

Hodge's and Warfield's theological method and doctrine of Scripture had significant influence beyond Princeton and Presbyterianism. Baptist students earned doctoral degrees under them and returned to teach in Baptist seminaries, bringing Princeton Theology with them. James Petrigu Boyce (1827–88), for example, studied theology under Charles Hodge at Princeton and went on to found Southern Baptist Theological Seminary in 1859. The influence of Princeton Theology is indelibly stamped on that seminary through the "Abstract of Principles" that Boyce wrote and all professors are required to sign. Methodists were relatively untouched by Princeton Theology as were many, if not most, turn-of-the-century revivalists in the Pentecostal-Holiness movement. Many evangelicals knew little or nothing of Princeton, its theology, and its theologians, but eventually the evangelical movement as a whole was touched by it through the last of the great Princeton School theologians, J. Gresham Machen.

---

[6]Ibid., 221.

Machen was one of Warfield's brightest students at Princeton during the first decade of the twentieth century. After completing graduate degrees at both Princeton University and Princeton Seminary, the Baltimore scholar studied New Testament and theology at two of Germany's leading universities—Marburg and Göttingen. He then served as instructor and professor of New Testament at his alma mater from 1906 until his departure to help found Westminster Theological Seminary in Philadelphia in 1929. Machen and some of his conservative colleagues believed that Princeton Seminary was departing from its true, historical heritage and succumbing to liberal influences. Westminster was to be the new home of "old school Princeton theology." In 1935 Machen was suspended from ministry by the Presbyterian Church because he helped found a conservative mission board rivaling the official board of the church, and in 1936 he helped found a new conservative denomination that eventually came to be called the Orthodox Presbyterian Church. Both Westminster Seminary and the Orthodox Presbyterian Church have exercised influence within Evangelicalism far beyond their sizes through conservative, Reformed theologians such as Machen, Cornelius Van Til, Gordon Clark, Harold John Ockenga, and Francis Schaeffer. Over the years both the seminary and denomination (which are not officially related to each other) suffered severe controversies and divisions as professors and ministers sought to preserve strict doctrinal orthodoxy against any and all deviations, real or imagined. One of militant, separatistic fundamentalism's most outspoken leaders, Carl McIntire (1906–2002), left both Westminster and the Orthodox Presbyterian Church rather noisily to found even more conservative Faith Theological Seminary and the Bible Presbyterian Church.

Machen's influence on Evangelicalism and evangelical theology is manifold. Without doubt he was a great scholar of the New Testament who knew his liberal opponents well. He studied under them and understood them before publishing his disagreements. Whereas Hodge and Warfield had been loyal opponents of the increasingly influential liberal mood of theology and biblical studies within the Presbyterian Church, Machen advocated division rather than compromise or coexistence. His little book *Christianity and Liberalism* (1923), a major splash on the theological scene, represented a manifesto of conservative Protestant Christianity against liberal theology, which the author described as a different religion from Christianity. The book pitted Machen's version of historic, orthodox Protestant Christianity (which was colored by Princeton Theology) against the mainline, liberal Protestant Christianity represented by influential ministers such as Harry Emerson Fosdick and left little room for a mediating, middle ground. Influential secular columnist and cultural commentator Walter Lippmann read Machen's manifesto and sided with it (without becoming a conservative himself, of course!). Machen's little volume appeared at the height of the great liberal-fundamentalist controversy that consumed several mainline denominations for several decades and eventually led to schisms within their ranks. Without doubt the book contributed to that situation by convincing many conservative evangelicals within the historic, mainline Protestant denominations—especially the Northern Baptist Convention and the Presbyterian Church in the U.S.A. ("Northern Presbyterian")—that they must leave those "apostate" churches.

The 1920s and 1930s probably saw the foundings of more new conservative denominations and new, independent, conservative Bible colleges than any other period of time in American history. Machen was hailed as a hero and embraced by fundamentalists everywhere, but he hardly fit the stereotypical image of fundamentalists promoted by writer H. L. Mencken, who portrayed them as ignorant, legalistic, and mean-spirited. Machen was a refined and reserved man of letters who saw nothing wrong with strong drink or smoking in moderation and was extremely uncomfortable at revival meetings. He believed that some combination of the theory of biological evolution with the Christian doctrine of creation was possible and had little use for the anti-evolution crusades launched and led by many fundamentalist leaders.

The Princeton School of theology from Alexander through Machen formed a kind of second pole to revivalism within Evangelicalism and evangelical theology. Revivalism, based on Pietism but going beyond it, created Evangelicalism in its awakenings, frontier revivals, mass evangelistic campaigns, and numerous spiritual retreats, conferences, and evangelistic networks. Its emphasis on *conversional* piety led evangelical theology to focus a great deal on salvation, including especially the experience of the new birth, the regenerating power of God through faith, and the progress of sanctification toward sinless perfection or "victorious Christian living." Princeton Theology, based on Puritanism but going beyond it, stamped Evangelicalism and evangelical theology with an emphasis on theological correctness and especially the foundations of orthodoxy in the doctrine of Scripture as supernaturally, verbally inspired and inerrant.

These two poles or impulses rest uneasily alongside each other within Evangelicalism and evangelical theology. One is passionate, relatively subjective (personal, inward, experience-oriented) and the other is cognitive, relatively objective (propositional, rational, intellectually oriented). During the last two decades of the nineteenth century and the first two decades of the twentieth century, many, if not most, North American Protestant Christians were coming increasingly under the influence of this dipolar Evangelicalism. Among Protestants, only Episcopalians and Lutherans were relatively untouched by either pole. Increasingly by the 1920s most Protestants of most denominations were finding the combination of the two poles irresistible. Wheaton College, perhaps the stackpole of evangelical higher education, begun under the influence of Finney-style revivalism in the middle of the nineteenth century, during the 1930s came increasingly under the influence of Princeton theology. Many churches and institutions dominated by Princeton-style conservative theology came to be influenced by revivalism.

8

Holiness-Pentecostalism and Evangelical Theology

Two movements that especially influenced Evangelicalism and evangelical theology in the twentieth century are the Holiness-Pentecostal movement and fundamentalism. Many people tend to equate them or subsume the former under the latter as an especially emotional form of fundamentalism. However, this is not correct. In spite of certain similarities, the Holiness-Pentecostal movement and fundamentalism moved on separate tracks. When the postfundamentalist "neo-evangelical" coalition was forged in the 1940s and 1950s, it left separatistic fundamentalism behind while retaining many fundamentalist concerns and habits. It embraced most of the Holiness-Pentecostal movement while shunning its most extreme forms and manifestations.

The Holiness-Pentecostal movement is older than funda-mentalism, so it will be described and discussed first. It grew out of revivalism in North America in the middle of the nineteenth century and may have been founded by a woman—Phoebe Palmer (1807–74). Palmer was a New York Methodist married to a medical doctor. In her thirties she became involved in a small group called the "Tuesday Meeting for the Promotion of Holiness" modeled after John and Charles Wesley's "Holy Club" at Oxford University. She studied Wesley's writings on sanctification and especially his *A Plain Account of Christian Perfection* and developed her own version of Methodist "entire sanctification," which she popularized through books such as *The Way of Holiness* and through a magazine entitled *Guide to Holiness*. Palmer led or preached in more than three hundred camp meetings and revivals throughout North America and Great Britain and without doubt was the single most influential personality in the rise of the Holiness movement, which stressed conversion, a "second blessing" subsequent to conver-sion called Spirit baptism or baptism of the Holy Spirit, and "holiness unto the Lord" through personal consecration to Jesus Christ and cleansing from the corruption of sin through the indwelling presence and power of the Holy Spirit. The New York Holiness revivalist developed a three-step process for ac-quiring entire sanctification known as "altar theology": entire consecration of oneself to God, trust in God to keep his prom-ise to sanctify that which is laid on the altar in consecration (the self), and witnessing to what God has done. This simple, straightforward method of sanctification caught on among many of the Methodist renewal offshoots and became a stan-dard formula holding the Holiness churches and organiza-tions together.

The Holiness movement emerged out of various indepen-dent organizations for renewal within the Methodist Episcopal Church and other Protestant denominations and some that had no denominational roots or affiliation. In 1867 these groups came together in a loose coalition known as the National Camp Meeting Association for the Promotion of Holiness or National Holiness Association. In 1971 the name of this umbrella organization was changed to the Christian Holiness Association. Although the association was mostly lay led and loosely organized, it helped give impetus to a growing movement that involved many small, new denominations, including the Church of the Nazarene, the Free Methodist Church, the Wesleyan Holiness Church, the Fire-Baptized Holiness Church, and the Church of God in Christ. Holiness people believed in the second blessing taught by Phoebe Palmer—the Spirit baptism for entire sanctification. They believed that the fallen, sinful nature could be cleansed and sinful urges and impulses eradicated in a moment so that from that time on the sanctified Christian would no longer struggle daily against temptation ("the flesh") or sin presumptuously. Such a person would, so Holiness preachers and teachers proclaimed, experience "Christian perfection," even though he or she would still commit sins of omission out of ignorance.

Camp meetings, conferences, and new churches centered around this experience sprang up all over North America and spread to other parts of the world through Holiness missions organizations. Perhaps the best-known Holiness denomination in the world is the Salvation Army, founded by Methodist Holiness social reformer William Booth in England in 1865. Many nineteenth-century Holiness Christians were social reformers in the forefronts of movements for equal rights for African Americans and women. Holiness denominations were among the first Christian churches to ordain women. When the new evangelical coalition emerged out of fundamentalism in the 1940s and 1950s, Holiness groups and leaders were involved; Free Methodists were among the founders of the National Association of Evangelicals.

Pentecostalism grew out of the wider Holiness movement in the first decade of the twentieth century.[1] "Wider" here indicates an influence of Holiness revivalism far beyond the specific boundaries of the National Holiness Association. Many North American and British revivalists of the later nineteenth century were proclaiming a "higher life" message that included a second-blessing experience subsequent to conversion that propels Christians into a more profound relationship with God through Jesus Christ and results in peace from the struggle between the spiritual side of the person and the world, the flesh, and the devil. This higher dimension of spiritual life, the revivalists taught, is initiated by a Spirit infilling or Spirit baptism, such as Jesus' disciples experienced on the day of Pentecost (Acts 2), and results in extraordinary power to live a consecrated life set apart unto God and to exercise the special, supernatural gifts of the Holy Spirit ("charismata") such as divine healing.

The Keswick movement, begun in Great Britain in 1876, emphasized higher Christian life through cessation of effort to live a life pleasing to God and replacement of that effort with complete emptiness of self and fullness of the Holy Spirit. Leaders of the Keswick movement, Great Britain's equivalent to the North American Holiness movement, included F. B. Meyer, Andrew Murray, and G. Campbell Morgan. Keswick teaching tended to be less emotional and somewhat more mystical than Holiness revivalism, but the basic impulse was the same—Christian perfectionism through Spirit baptism. In New York and New England two American revivalists of the later nineteenth and early twentieth centuries especially laid the groundwork for Pentecostalism: A. J. Gordon (1836–95) and

---

[1]For an account of the rise of Pentecostalism see Harvey Cox, *Fire from Heaven: The Rise of Pentecostal Spirituality and the Reshaping of Religion in the Twenty-First Century* (Reading, MA: Addison-Wesley Publishing Co., 1995).

A. B. Simpson (1843–1919). Through their devotional writings, preaching, conference teaching, and hymns, these men promoted a popular version of Keswick higher-life theology that focused on the infilling of the Holy Spirit for power over sin and power for Christian service. A. B. Simpson, who founded a new denomination known as the Christian and Missionary Alliance, taught that divine healing was provided for by Christ's atoning death on the cross and that faith-filled prayer for healing should be a normal aspect of higher-life Christianity.

By the dawn of the new century in 1901, the North American Holiness movement was at its peak of popularity and fervor and Holiness ideas about the second blessing, entire sanctification, higher life, divine healing, and the infilling of the Holy Spirit as an enduement with power for all Christians were permeating evangelical Christianity in many denominations and among nondenominational Christians. Holiness camp meetings, protracted revivals, higher-life conferences, and Bible training institutes were cropping up all over North America. Out of this milieu emerged the Pentecostal movement. The precise date of its birth is debated by scholars. Some argue that it was born at the moment of the birth of the twentieth century—midnight, January 1, 1901. At that moment (or near it) a woman student at a Holiness Bible institute in Topeka, Kansas, spoke in tongues as she received the second-blessing experience of Spirit baptism. The founder of Topeka's Bethel Bible School, Charles Parham, interpreted speaking in tongues as the "initial, physical evidence" of the baptism of the Holy Spirit and spread the message of this special sign of the "latter rain" (of God's Spirit upon all flesh) throughout North America. Other Holiness revivalists took up that message and speaking in tongues became for many Holiness Christians the sine qua non of higher Christian life. Some scholars date the birth of Pentecostalism to the Azusa Street Revival in Los Angeles, California, in 1906 led by African American Holiness evangelist

William Seymour. The revival lasted for months, and thousands of Holiness Christians flocked to it from everywhere to witness what was happening as people prophesied, spoke in tongues, claimed divine healing. Many of them went back to their home churches with the new sign of Spirit baptism.

Some Holiness Christians accepted the Pentecostal message—sometimes called the "Full Gospel"—and some did not. Several Holiness denominations split over it; others converted completely to it. The predominantly African American Church of God in Christ became Pentecostal. White Pentecostal leaders founded the Assemblies of God denomination in 1914. They disagreed with the Holiness distinctive of entire sanctification but agreed with A. B. Simpson about Spirit baptism and divine healing. They expected Simpson to join the new movement, but instead he published his policy toward speaking in tongues as "Seek not; forbid not," and his Christian and Missionary Alliance denomination split. Many of the white founders of Pentecostalism in North America were former followers of Simpson.

Pentecostalism represented an intense form of revivalism. Its theological underpinnings were the same as those of other orthodox Arminian Protestant Christian groups, although the movement divided over the doctrine of the Trinity early in its history. Some Pentecostals rejected orthodox Trinitarianism in favor of a "Oneness" message that reduced the persons of the Trinity to manifestations of one person. This branch of Pentecostalism, sometimes known as Jesus Only or Oneness Pentecostalism, was rejected by the majority and never played any significant role in Evangelicalism. Above and beyond basic Protestant orthodoxy, however, Pentecostals embraced the higher-life message of A. B. Simpson and/or the Holiness message of Phoebe Palmer and the National Holiness Association. Some Pentecostals believe in entire sanctification and some do not; all believe in the experience of second blessing of Spirit baptism or Spirit infilling for all Christians with the accompanying, verifying sign of speaking in tongues. They base this doctrine on a perceived pattern in the New Testament book of Acts in which early converts to Christianity spoke in tongues and prophesied when they were filled with the Holy Spirit. Nearly all Pentecostals adopted a theology borrowed from A. B. Simpson: the so-called "foursquare gospel" of Jesus Christ as Savior (including his deity, lordship, and blood atonement for remission of sins); Baptizer with the Holy Spirit (including his special indwelling presence for power for holy living and Christian service); Healer (including his provision for physical healing in his atoning death on the cross and by his bodily resurrection from the dead); and Coming King (including his imminent, visible return to establish his kingdom on earth). Like the Holiness movement from which it emerged, Pentecostalism is thoroughly Arminian in its theology of salvation, emphasizing not divine sovereignty in predestination but instead proclaiming unlimited atonement and every person's ability to respond freely to the gospel unto salvation.

The Holiness-Pentecostal movement that flourished between the mid-nineteenth century and the mid-twentieth century (and still exists and grows) was intensely experiential and emotional. It tended to downplay theological correctness and doctrinal precision, as well as intellectual inquiry in general. Some scholars have argued that it was and remains severely anti-intellectual and otherworldly in ethos, even though in the later part of the twentieth century some genuine biblical and theological scholarship has arisen from within its ranks. Its emphasis on emotional experiences, miracles, rejection of "worldliness" in appearance and amusement, and imminent return of Christ gained it the pejorative descriptor "Holy Rollers" and caused even many evangelical Christians to reject it as fanatical. B. B. Warfield published a scholarly volume against the movement entitled *Counterfeit Miracles,* and many conservative

Protestants argued that the so-called "sign gifts" of the Holy Spirit such as divine healing, prophecy, and speaking in tongues ceased when the canon of inspired Scripture was completed (cessationism).

Throughout the first half of the twentieth century, Pentecostalism especially languished in a limbo state in relation to the rest of conservative, evangelical Protestant Christianity. It was harshly condemned by nearly everyone, including its own Holiness and higher-life cousins. When the National Association of Evangelicals was formed in 1942, however, the decision was made to include both Holiness and Pentecostal denominations. The Free Methodist Church and the Assemblies of God were both among its charter members, and leaders of those two groups served on the NAE's board in later years. By the 1970s and 1980s Holiness and Pentecostal Christians were in the thick of Evangelicalism in North America, and their influence on evangelical worship, spirituality, and doctrine has been noticeable. They have always remained, however, a distinct subset of Evangelicalism. The vast majority of evangelicals have never embraced either entire sanctification or speaking in tongues. The legacy of the Holiness-Pentecostal movement to evangelical theology is an emphasis on higher spiritual life—especially second-blessing-type experiences subsequent to conversion—and interest in the gifts of the Holy Spirit. While many evangelical Christians have little or no use for emotional displays of spirituality, almost all have been affected by the renewal of the doctrine of the Holy Spirit and the Spirit's work in the Christian life introduced by Holiness-Pentecostal revivalists. So-called contemporary worship (chorus singing with arms raised, hand clapping to energetic "praise and worship" choruses, informal worship) is an obvious extension of certain worship styles that were born in the Holiness-Pentecostal meetings of the turn of the century. Another possible legacy of Holiness-Pentecostalism to the wider

evangelical community is an active disinterest in rigorous biblical and theological study, doctrine, and evangelical intellectual creativity and participation in the wider culture.[2]

---

[2]See Mark A. Noll, *The Scandal of the Evangelical Mind* (Grand Rapids:
Wm. B. Eerdmans, 1994).

9

Fundamentalism and Evangelical Theology

In the immediate background of Evangelicalism and evangelical theology lies fundamentalism or the fundamentalist movement. Some untutored religious journalists and commentators tend to equate fundamentalism with Evangelicalism in an overly simplistic way. The connection is correct, but a distinction is important. Some people tend to equate fundamentalism with revivalism in general. Again, there is a connection, but there is also an important distinction. *Fundamentalism* is a term used correctly to describe three distinct but interrelated religious phenomena. During the 1970s many journalists and scholars began to use the term *fundamentalism* to describe any and all militant religious reactions to modernity.[1] By modernity

---

[1] See *The Fundamentalism Project,* 7 vols., ed. Scott Appleby and Martin Marty (Chicago: University of Chicago Press, 1991–95).

they mean the secularizing impulses that began with the scientific revolution of the seventeenth and eighteenth centuries and with its philosophical counterpart in the cultural revolution known as the Enlightenment. In this sense, fundamentalism includes militantly antimodern conservatives within all world religions. This fairly recent, generally secular journalistic definition of *fundamentalism* is not used here.

An older and more historically correct meaning of fundamentalism is the conservative Protestant reaction to the rise of liberal Protestantism in the later decades of the nineteenth century and early decades of the twentieth century. All such fundamentalists also called themselves evangelicals and regarded themselves as guardians and defenders of evangelical truth in an increasingly secularized and liberal theological world. In this sense, B. B. Warfield and his student J. Gresham Machen were fundamentalists. So were many, if not nearly all, conservative evangelicals of the first few decades of the twentieth century. A few evangelical groups sat out the so-called liberal-fundamentalist conflict that raged within mainline Protestantism at that time. They tended to be immigrant Pietist churches and Holiness-Pentecostals.

A third, more historically legitimate, definition of *fundamentalism* is the narrower, more militant and separatistic movement of conservative Protestants that emerged out of disappointment and despair in the 1920s and 1930s, as the major Protestant denominations of North America were lost for conservative theology and became increasingly liberal and pluralistic. The difference between early fundamentalism and later fundamentalism is not so much one of doctrine as of mood. The single most important distinction between them has to do with later fundamentalism's adoption of a militant stance toward exposing the "heresies" of other Christians and of a policy of separation not only from liberal Christians but also from fellow evangelicals who do not separate from liberal Christian denominations and organizations.[2]

Scholars do not agree on the precise beginnings of early Christian fundamentalism. The term itself arose in stages. Some conservative Protestants were talking about the need to reaffirm the "fundamentals of the faith" in the 1890s as they became aware of the influence of higher criticism of the Bible (i.e., literary criticism) in their denomination's seminaries. In direct response to perceived destructive biblical scholarship within those seminaries, conservative Protestants began to organize Bible conferences around the country where speakers explored biblical themes and exhorted listeners to take the Bible literally as God's Word. One such influential Bible conference, the Niagara Bible Conference, began in the 1860s (before moving to Niagara-on-the-Lake, Ontario) and lasted until 1897. Each year thousands of pastors and lay Christians flocked to the summer conference at Niagara-on-the-Lake in Ontario, Canada, to hear prominent conservative biblical teachers and expositors teach about subjects such as the second coming of Jesus Christ and the importance of biblical inerrancy. In 1878 the conference produced a list of essentials of authentic Christian belief—the "Niagara Creed"—which may have been the first list of "fundamentals" other than the historic creeds and confessions of Christianity and the Reformation. It included biblical inerrancy and the "personal and premillennial advent" of Jesus Christ. After that, many such lists of fundamentals were proposed by conservative Protestants in reaction to the rise of liberalism within their denominations. Most such lists included biblical inspiration and inerrancy, the virgin birth of Christ (because it was increasingly under attack by liberals of the "new theology"), Christ's resurrection, salvation by the blood atone-

---

[2]See Alan P. F. Sell, *Theology in Turmoil: The Roots, Course, and Significance of the Conservative-Liberal Debate in Modern Theology* (Grand Rapids: Baker Book House, 1986).

ment of Christ on the cross, and Christ's second coming.

The term *fundamentalism* may derive from a set of booklets entitled *The Fundamentals,* published between 1910 and 1915 and sent free of charge to all Protestant ministers, church workers, and YMCA directors by two California businessmen. The booklets contained articles on the Bible, doctrine, and controversial issues by leading conservative theological scholars such as B. B. Warfield, Southern Baptist seminary president and theologian E. Y. Mullins, Scottish theologian James Orr. The first use of the labels *fundamentalist* and *fundamentalism,* however, appeared in 1920 in the magazine *Baptist Watchman-Examiner,* whose editor, Curtis Lee Laws, coined them to designate conservative Protestant orthodoxy in contrast to liberal, modernist theology that was skeptical toward traditional doctrines and miracles. Around the same time, a leading conservative Baptist minister, William Bell Riley (1861–1947) of Minneapolis, Minnesota, founded the World's Christian Fundamentals Association to counter liberalism's influence. By the mid-1920s *fundamentalism* was a widely used term for relatively aggressive conservatism in Protestant theology in North America.

The early fundamentalists may have been very conservative in almost every sense, but they were not militant or separatistic. They remained within their mainline Protestant denominations, hoping to reform them away from debilitating modernism (i.e., overaccommodation to the skeptical spirit of the modern age) toward what they regarded as historic Protestant orthodoxy. This would be true especially of the great Scottish Presbyterian theologian James Orr (1844–1913), who made several trips to the United States to give lectures and aid in the conservative effort to stem the tide of liberal theology. His books *The Christian View of God and the World* (1893) and *The Ritschlian Theology and the Evangelical Faith* (1897) represented scholarly critiques of liberal theology without harsh polemics or narrow, sectarian presentations of Protestant orthodoxy. Orr never did advocate belief in the inerrancy of the Bible; yet he was embraced by American fundamentalists as an ally in the cause. Later fundamentalists would reject fellowship with anyone who, like Orr and other early conservative Protestant scholars, did not wholeheartedly affirm biblical inerrancy and other peculiar beliefs such as a pretribulational rapture of the church (dispensationalism). J. Gresham Machen was another early fundamentalist who, although quite conservative and a true believer in biblical inerrancy, tried to keep the antiliberal crusade among conservatives focused on true essentials of Christian belief. However, his *Christianity and Liberalism,* along with his own departure from Princeton Seminary and the Presbyterian Church, gave impetus to the development of later "second-stage" fundamentalism with its militancy of rhetoric and separatistic behavior.

Several developments in the battle between conservatives and liberals for control of America's major Protestant institutions in the 1920s resulted in the rise of later, second-stage fundamentalism. The famous Scopes "monkey trial" in Dayton, Tennessee, in 1925 convinced many fundamentalists that American culture—including the media and church institutions—was set against them. The Northern Baptist Convention and the Presbyterian Church in the U.S.A. took firm stands against exclusion of moderates and liberals from their ministerial ranks. Leading Protestant seminaries such as the University of Chicago's Divinity School and Union Theological Seminary in New York fell decisively into the liberal camp. Liberal preacher Harry Emerson Fosdick Jr. appeared on the cover of *Time* magazine and was widely applauded for his stand against fundamentalism. To many fundamentalists, all this was sure evidence of the apostasy of the American mainline Protestant denominations.

Like many disillusioned Puritans in seventeenth-century

England, the fundamentalists began to harden their own categories and exit mainline Protestantism to found smaller, archconservative, rival denominations and institutions. William Bell Riley (1861–1947), a leading warhorse of fundamentalism, led the transition between the movement's early and later manifestations. He added belief in the premillennial return of Christ (i.e., belief in a literal one-thousand-year kingdom of God on earth after Christ's return) to his organization's list of fundamentals of Christianity and began to urge separation of true conservative Christians from all doctrinally reduced or polluted denominations and organizations. His own Northern Baptist Convention divided many times as fundamentalists of different types and degrees broke away to found new Baptist groups. The same happened in the Presbyterian Church and, to a lesser extent, in the Methodist Episcopal Church and the American Congregational Church. Almost overnight numerous new fundamentalist denominations, organizations, and institutions sprang up. Fundamentalist leaders such as John R. Rice, Bob Jones, and Carl McIntire criticized fellow conservatives who would not leave the mainline churches or who remained in any kind of Christian cooperation or fellowship with them.

Second-stage fundamentalists by and large condemned not only belief in evolution (including theistic evolution) but also "compromise" with "Godless evolution," which is how they regarded any attempt to accommodate Christian belief about origins with modern science. They adopted in whole or in part the relatively new approach to biblical interpretation and the end times known as dispensationalism and insisted that faithfulness to Scripture required belief in a literal millennium, if not a "secret rapture" of the church before a seven-year "tribulation period" at the end of history as we know it. They developed belief in and practice of "secondary separation," which means rejecting cooperation and fellowship with even fellow evangelicals who did not remain separated from "apostate" liberals in the mainline churches. Their formal or informal lists of fundamentals (essentials) of Christian belief and practice grew until little remained to private interpretation or opinion. Many of the leading fundamentalists were willing, if not eager, to support segregation of the races, anti-Catholicism in public speech and policy, and extreme right-wing politics. With regard to the doctrine of Scripture, at least some of them reverted past Princeton orthodoxy to blatant advocacy of a dictation theory of the Bible's origins. John R. Rice, for example, wrote that "God raised up men, prepared the men and prepared their vocabularies, and God dictated the very words which they would put down in the Scriptures." The spirit of second-stage fundamentalism is conveyed clearly in Rice's harsh criticism of anyone who disagreed with him: "Shame! So you want big prophets and a little God, do you? You do not want a man simply hearing what God says and writing it down, do you? Well, then, your attitude is simply the carnal attitude of the unbelieving world that always wants to give man credit instead of God, whether for salvation or inspiration."[3]

Many evangelical Protestant Christians who were not of the same militant, separatistic spirit as men like Riley, Jones, Rice, and McIntire continued to call themselves fundamentalists throughout the 1930s and 1940s. But the label became more and more problematic for anyone who wished to be taken seriously as thoughtful, reflective, and even relatively gentle and open-minded. By the beginning of the 1940s many conservative, evangelical Protestants in North America and Great Britain were disillusioned with the course and cause of second-stage fundamentalism and wanted to reform it. Such reform of fundamentalism began with the founding of a new organiza-

---

[3]Quoted in Donald K. McKim, *What Christians Believe About the Bible* (Nashville: Thomas Nelson Publishers, 1985), 57.

tion by a leading moderately fundamentalist Protestant minister named Harold John Ockenga (1904–85), who pastored influential Park Street Congregational Church in Boston, Massachusetts. Together with several other prominent conservatives who were disillusioned with separatistic fundamentalism, Ockenga formed the New England Fellowship to be a panevangelical alliance transcending narrow, sectarian boundaries. In 1942 the National Association of Evangelicals emerged out of the New England Fellowship and postfundamentalist, new Evangelicalism was born.

10

Introducing Postfundamentalist Evangelical Theology

The Evangelicalism that forms the context for this resource on evangelical theology is the postfundamentalist, new evangelical coalition that came into existence as a result of the efforts of Ockenga and his colleagues in the 1940s. Of course, they did not create an entire new religious movement. Instead, they managed to reform the fundamentalist movement by giving it a new face, so to speak. They reorganized and refurbished it and pushed out to its periphery those militant, separatistic leaders who had captivated it throughout the 1930s.[1] The latter continued to exist, of course, and so the two movements—later fundamentalism (militant, separatistic) and the new Evangelicalism (irenic, cooperative)—have existed alongside each other since

---

[1]Joel Carpenter, *Revive Us Again: The Reawakening of American Fundamentalism* (New York and Oxford: Oxford University Press, 1997).

then as the two wings of conservative Protestant Christianity. Eventually Jerry Falwell of Lynchburg, Virginia, emerged as the new spokesman for fundamentalism, even as Billy Graham emerged as the spokesman for Evangelicalism. They believe most of the same doctrines, but their approaches to culture and the churches are very different.

When Ockenga and his colleagues were organizing the National Association of Evangelicals (NAE) in 1942, Carl McIntire and some of his fundamentalist colleagues were organizing a rival, more separatistic umbrella organization called the American Council of Churches (later the International Council of Christian Churches). Talks were held between the two groups to see if they could merge as one evangelical-fundamentalist alliance of churches, but the NAE's inclusion of the Holiness-Pentecostal groups was a stumbling block for McIntire, who considered Pentecostals deluded. More importantly, however, Ockenga's group had visions of a "broad tent Evangelicalism" that would include as many conversionist, conservative Protestants as possible—not so much to fight liberalism in the mainline churches (which had their own Federal Council of Churches), but to coordinate activities among evangelicals and provide a greater evangelical witness to culture at large. The NAE charter and vision were too broad for McIntire and most other fundamentalists, so the merger never occurred.

The NAE produced a minimal statement of faith and adopted as its motto "In essentials unity, in non-essentials liberty, in all things charity [love]." While belief in Scripture's inspiration and authority are required, NAE does not require belief in inerrancy of the Bible or in premillennialism. Membership has been very diverse, including Reformed (Calvinist) churches, Arminian and Wesleyan denominations, Adventist groups, and many Holiness and Pentecostal denominations. One holdover from its fundamentalist beginnings is the exclusion of organizations already affiliated with the Federal

Council of Churches/National Council of Churches—the mostly liberal, mainline ecumenical organization.

The new Evangelicalism desperately needed a figurehead and a leading theological spokesman. It also needed a seminary and a publication. By the early 1950s a young evangelist named Billy Graham was emerging as the movement's figurehead, and by the mid-1950s its leading theologian was Carl F. H. Henry. Fuller Theological Seminary became its seminary and *Christianity Today* its publication. These forces, funded largely by contributions from wealthy evangelical businessman Howard Pew, held the fledgling postfundamentalist movement together in spite of tremendous inner tensions and conflicts.

Some new evangelicals were and are strong believers in biblical inerrancy; others are not. All believe in supernatural inspiration of Scripture, but some prefer to leave the nature of that process mysterious, while others believe it is important to describe it in terms of Warfield's "plenary, verbal inspiration." Some new evangelicals were and are five-point Calvinists (total depravity, unconditional election, limited atonement, irresistible grace, perseverance of the saints); others are Arminians and even open theists (God's limited foreknowledge). Some are passionate premillennialists and even dispensationalists; others are amillennialists, and a few are postmillennialists. Some are Pentecostals and charismatics; others are cessationists. Some believe in church hierarchy and high liturgy; others insist on the autonomy of the local congregation and prefer worship that is extremely informal.

Ockenga and his colleagues in the forging of the new evangelical coalition wanted all these diverse types of evangelicals to coexist and cooperate with each other in a loose network of evangelical fellowship. Due to the diversity within Evangelicalism, Ockenga's vision seemed doomed to fail until a single powerful leader with a strong organization emerged to hold it together around a common, unifying mission. That person was

Billy Graham (William Frank Graham, b. 1918). The organization was the Billy Graham Evangelistic Association, and the mission was Christian world evangelism, interpreted not only as individual spiritual salvation but also as permeation of the whole world, including social structures, with the gospel of Jesus Christ. Billy Graham's influence on Evangelicalism and evangelical theology is beyond calculation. It is doubtful whether either one would exist without him and his ministry. Graham's twin themes have provided the dual focus of Evangelicalism and evangelical theology in their postfundamentalist manifestation: conversion to Christ through personal repentance and faith in his cross, and the Bible as God's specially revealed Word, wholly inspired and completely trustworthy in all matters related to faith and practice. Of course evangelical theologians have gone far beyond merely exploring those two themes, but they have together provided the unifying foci of evangelical thought, witness, and work.

Fuller Theological Seminary was founded in 1947 by Ockenga with the inspiration and provision of California evangelist Charles E. Fuller. It was to become the premier, transdenominational evangelical seminary. *Christianity Today* was started in 1956 by Billy Graham and his father-in-law, L. Nelson Bell, with financial support from Howard Pew. It was to become the evangelical counterpart and rival to the more liberal *Christian Century* magazine and provide a conservative alternative to such fundamentalist publications as John R. Rice's *Sword of the Lord.* Carl F. H. Henry (1913–2003) was a conservative Baptist doctoral student at Boston University who became a founding faculty member at Fuller Theological Seminary and then founding editor of *Christianity Today.* He went on to publish numerous articles and books expounding the new evangelical theology. An article in *Time,* February 4, 1977, declared him "the leading theologian of the nation's growing Evangelical flank." Henry has often also been called the "dean of evangelical theologians."

Evangelicalism came to include many more publications, institutions, theologians, organizations, and ministries, but its path was determined by these early pioneers and symbols. Other leading movers and shakers of postfundamentalist evangelical theology—the theology of the postfundamentalist evangelical coalition—have included Henry's colleague and Ockenga's successor as president of Fuller Theological Seminary Edward John (E. J.) Carnell, Baptist theologian Bernard Ramm, Congregationalist-Presbyterian thinker Donald G. Bloesch, and postconservative evangelical theologian Clark Pinnock. While there have been and are many other evangelical thinkers who have contributed to the postfundamentalist evangelical movement's theology, these five theologians represent the best and are the most influential of all.

11

Carl F. H. Henry
Dean of Evangelical Theologians

Carl Henry's overriding concern throughout his theological career was to expound and defend what he saw as a distinctly evangelical view of theological method, including especially a view of divine revelation as the sole, supreme authority for Christian faith and practice. He argued, of course, that this evangelical approach to method and authority is the same as that of the classical Protestant Reformation. The only difference is that it is updated for twentieth-century (and now twenty-first century) Christians using modern tools of logical analysis and comparing and contrasting it with modern philosophical and theological alternatives. The *Time* article about Henry in 1977 was entitled "Theology for the Tent Meeting." The title writer apparently knew little of the evangelical theologian's thought. While Henry did not eschew the right kind of revivalism, he was never particularly friendly to attitudes toward belief often inspired by revivalists and embraced by those who attend tent revivals. His theological thinking was the antithesis of emotionalism, subjectivism, fideism, and obscurantism. To Henry, these are the bane of evangelical existence and need correction, if not rejection, by modern evangelical theologians. Henry's pattern of evangelical thinking escapes simple labeling, but one appropriate term for it may be "rational, evangelical, theistic presuppositionalism."

Behind Henry's thinking stands the shaping influence of a highly rationalistic philosopher, Gordon Clark (1902–86). Clark was Henry's philosophy instructor at Wheaton College in the 1930s. Henry later called him "one of the profoundest evangelical Protestant philosophers of our time." Clark was an ardent Calvinist who believed that logic provided the God-given key to thinking God's thoughts after him and arriving at *A Christian View of Men and Things*—the title of one of his most influential books (1951). Henry took up Clark's philosophy, which centered around the critical uses of presuppositions and logical deduction in eliminating all but conservative, evangelical Protestant belief from the realm of possibility. He attempted to show that without belief in a personal God who "speaks and shows" in propositional, inerrant divine revelation, any and every human belief system (set of answers to life's ultimate questions) will inevitably end up in nihilism (belief in the ultimate absurdity of existence), which is itself contradictory. Like his mentor Clark, Henry wielded the law of noncontradiction to dissect and reduce to absurdity every non-Christian worldview and theology—including especially liberal Protestantism.

Henry's theology, then, was not exactly what one expects from a "theology for the tent meeting," and it has been criticized by some of Henry's evangelical colleagues as too rationalistic. Nevertheless, it has influenced a large number of evangelical theologians, pastors, and lay leaders, especially through Henry's columns in *Christianity Today*, which he edited for over a decade and served as contributing editor for almost a decade after his retirement in 1968. Henry's books tend to be weighty theological tomes—even when they are relatively brief. His

Towards a Recovery of Christian Belief (Wheaton, IL: Crossway Books, 1990) comprises only 120 pages but, like most of Henry's writings, is a challenge to the mind of the reader. His magnum opus is a seven-volume work on theological method and divine revelation entitled *God, Revelation, and Authority* (Waco, TX: Word, 1976–84). Few persons, if any, could claim to have read all of it. And yet the wide use of individual volumes of the set as textbooks in evangelical colleges, universities, and seminaries has influenced thousands of evangelical students who went on to become ministers and denominational and parachurch leaders and teachers.

Carl Ferdinand Howard Henry was born to German immigrant parents in New York City on January 22, 1913, and experienced a "great awakening" or conversion to Jesus Christ at the age of twenty. After his Christian conversion he attended Wheaton College, the mecca of progressive fundamentalist higher education in the 1930s. Billy Graham would attend it soon after Henry. Numerous other evangelicals who helped form the postfundamentalist evangelical coalition went through Wheaton College, where they were shaped by a rigorously intellectual faculty and a theology of "generous orthodoxy." There Henry fell under the influence of Gordon Clark and drank deeply of what has been called by some critics "the evangelical enlightenment." That is, Clark's philosophy focused on the need for rational certainty about God that left little room for faith other than as a personal trust in what reason could prove. Some critics have found in it—and in other, similar evangelical approaches to philosophy and theology—an echo, if not an influence, of René Descartes's Enlightenment rationalism. Clark had little use for any epistemological role for the Holy Spirit, such as the traditional Calvinist "internal testimony of the Holy Spirit." He believed and taught that the classical Protestant Christian belief system (without the epistemological role of the Holy Spirit as authenticating power of the truth of divine revelation) could be demonstrated to be rationally superior to all competing, alternative belief systems including naturalism, absolute idealism, pantheism, and humanism.

After graduating from Wheaton College, Henry attended Northern Baptist Theological Seminary in Chicago and was ordained a Baptist minister. After seminary he pursued a Ph.D. in theology from the University of Boston, where he studied with philosopher of religion Edgar Sheffield Brightman, one of the founders of the liberal Personalist school of theology. His doctoral dissertation, entitled "Personal Idealism and Strong's Theology," was a critical study of turn-of-the-century mediating Baptist theologian Augustus Hopkins Strong's theology. Henry attempted to show the influence of early Personalist philosophy on Strong's thought. Strong had been and remained for many years after Henry's dissertation the single most influential theologian among conservative Protestants after Charles Hodge. Strong's three-volume 1907 *Systematic Theology* was widely used in free-church colleges and seminaries as the basic textbook of evangelical thought. It was generally considered conservative and Calvinistic, although not as congenial to fundamentalism as Hodge's three-volume *Systematic Theology*. Strong was more open to theistic evolution than Hodge or his most faithful followers, and he promoted a "dynamical theory" of inspiration of Scripture that differed significantly from Hodge's plenary, verbal theory. Also, Strong believed that errors in "secular matters" in Scripture would not undermine its inspiration and infallibility, which he regarded as having to do with Scripture as "a textbook of religion." While an irenic treatment of Strong's theology, Henry's dissertation served to undermine its influence among progressive fundamentalists (it had little or no influence among separatistic fundamentalists), who would eventually become postfundamentalist evangelicals, by purporting to show alien philosophical elements in it.

While he was working on his doctorate, Henry taught part-time at evangelical Gordon College in suburban Boston and helped found Fuller Theological Seminary with Ockenga and a group of progressive fundamentalists from the United States and Great Britain. This group became the nucleus of the post-fundamentalist evangelical movement. Originally, their main concern was to establish conservative, conversionist Protestant thought on a less separatistic, less anti-intellectual foundation than fundamentalism. They were disillusioned with their own fundamentalist coalition and its theology, which they thought had degenerated into militancy, sectarianism, and fideism. In 1949 Henry helped found the Evangelical Theological Society, whose only confessional requirement for membership was biblical inerrancy. The stated purpose of the society was to combat liberal theology without embracing fundamentalism.

Many commentators on postfundamentalist Evangelicalism regard Henry's *The Uneasy Conscience of Modern Fundamentalism* (1947) the first neo-evangelical (i.e., postfundamentalist evangelical) book. In it the young evangelical theologian criticized fundamentalism for neglecting the social world outside the confines of the separated church. Fundamentalism—including almost all evangelicals—had been in sharp reaction against the social gospel movement that arose with liberal theology in the late nineteenth and early twentieth centuries. As Donald W. Dayton and other evangelical historians have shown, evangelicals in the nineteenth century—especially prior to the Civil War—had been social reformers.[1] Some had been quite radical abolitionists and practiced civil disobedience. Evangelicals were once in the forefront of progressive social change, but all that changed with the revivalism of D. L. Moody and later Billy Sunday. They and other evangelical revivalists were strongly premillennial and pessimistic about changing the structures of

---

[1]Donald W. Dayton, *Rediscovering an Evangelical Heritage* (Peabody, MA: Hendrickson Publishers, 1988).

society. Early fundamentalism was wary of the social gospel movement of men like Washington Gladden and Walter Rauschenbusch because it was closely associated with and greatly influenced by the liberal Protestant thinking of German theologian Albrecht Ritschl and his followers.

Henry's book, then, fell like a bombshell on conservative Protestantism in North America as he called fundamentalism (by which he still at that time meant conservative Protestantism in general) to repent of its indifference to social sin and become involved once again in helping to ameliorate the effects of sin in the social order. Because separatistic fundamentalists reacted negatively to the book, while it was hailed by many moderate evangelicals, *The Uneasy Conscience of Modern Fundamentalism* came to be viewed as a neo-evangelical manifesto decisively breaking the new evangelical movement away from its older fundamentalist roots.

Overall and in general, however, Henry's career in theology was conservative. He sought to warn fellow evangelicals (and anyone else who would listen) of the poison of subjectivism in philosophy and theology, and his focus returned again and again to fighting that poison as he believed it appeared in and corrupted Christianity. The two main examples of subjectivism's deleterious affects are, in Henry's analysis, liberal Protestantism and neo-orthodoxy. The former, Henry claimed, represents near capitulation to the modern secular spirit of the age that elevates the autonomous reasoning of sinful humanity to godlike status and removes religion, including Christianity, from its rational foundation onto the shifting sands of "common human religious experience"—whether intuitional (as in Schleiermacher) or ethical (as in Ritschl). The liberals came to view the Bible, Henry claimed, as little more than representation of universal human sentiments about God and humanity. In their hands it lost its authority as the governing norm of Christian faith and practice, precisely because liberals gave up belief in its supernatural divine origin in verbal inspiration and denied its inerrancy.

Neo-orthodoxy came in for special criticism from Henry because in his view it is such a seductive alternative to Protestant orthodoxy; many evangelicals, once loosed from the iron grip of militant, separatistic fundamentalism, turned to major neo-orthodox thinkers such as Karl Barth and Emil Brunner for guidance in rethinking theological method and the nature of divine revelation and Scripture.[2] According to neo-orthodoxy or, as many of its proponents prefer to call it, dialectical theology, divine revelation is supernatural (contrary to liberal theology) but nonpropositional. That is, according to Barth and Brunner and their colleagues and disciples, when God reveals he reveals only *himself* and never *information about himself*. Revelation, so neo-orthodoxy seems to say, is personal, historical, and dialogical, not rational, propositional, or cognitive. At least this is how Henry interpreted neo-orthodoxy.

The upshot is that Henry surveyed the theological scene in the 1950s through the 1990s and thought he noticed *one, single, main disease* infecting and corrupting Christian theology: *anti-intellectualism*—a "flight from reason." Fundamentalism's brand of anti-intellectualism was obvious to Henry, and he felt little need to expose it at great length or in great detail. The fundamentalism of the 1920s and since had fallen into obscurantist isolation from the world of thought and cared little about the life of the mind outside of its own esoteric biblical studies, such as detailed examination of the biblical apocalyptic prophecies of the end times and reading the "signs of the times" to detect when Christ might return.

Liberal theology's brand of anti-intellectualism was more

---

[2]For an examination of the influence of Karl Barth, the leading neo-orthodox theologian, on evangelicals and evangelical theology, see Gregory C. Bolich, *Karl Barth and Evangelicalism* (Downers Grove, IL: InterVarsity Press, 1980).

subtle, and Henry endeavored to expose it in many of his writings. According to his critical analysis, liberal Protestant theology had begun rejecting rigorous rational and intellectual activity in theology with Schleiermacher's emphasis on universal religious feeling as the basis for even Christian theology and had continued its anti-intellectual project with Ritschl's divorce between "facts" and "values"—relegating religious and theological judgments to the latter realm. As a result, Christian theology became little more than an extension of mystical intuition, with no objective truth content, or else an extension of universal human moral intuition, in which case it still has no objective truth content.

Neo-orthodoxy, Henry complained, is guilty of its own anti-intellectualism because it denies objective divine revelation of information, revels in paradoxes if not contradictions, and rejects the Bible as supernaturally verbally inspired and inerrant. For neo-orthodoxy, the Bible "becomes the Word of God" in the mysterious, unpredictable encounter between God and the human person. Henry regarded that as undermining the Bible as an objective authority for critically examining teaching and constructing sound doctrine. The upshot of all these forms of twentieth-century theology, Henry argued, is a noncognitive, anti-intellectual, subjective Christian faith that cannot sustain its public prophetic role of teaching truth about God.

Henry's proposed cure for all of modern theology's ills is a theological "back to the Bible movement" in which Scripture is once again understood as a propositional, verbally inspired and inerrant revelation of God that communicates a life and worldview logically and experientially superior to all alternatives. Henry's theology has a decidedly apologetic thrust. He was interested in demonstrating the rational superiority of Protestant orthodoxy over all competing theologies and worldviews, but he believed the key to such a project and to putting Christian theology on a sound foundation is proper presuppositions ("axioms") and correct logical deduction.

Every comprehensive system of belief, Henry averred, rests
on unprovable axioms. In order for reasonable discourse (dialogue, debate, proclamation) to take place, there must be certain universally agreed-on axioms that transcend particular belief systems. For example, if a person does not agree that
"[t]here can be but one comprehensive system of truth,"[3] that
person either does not understand the meaning of "comprehensive system of truth" or is wrongheaded. It is impossible to
communicate reasonably with such a person about matters of
ultimate meaning—that is, truth claims about ultimate reality.
Henry was interested only in universal, absolute truth; he considered all forms of relativism self-contradictory and therefore
anti-intellectual. It is strictly impossible to discuss truth without
agreement about its nature as unified correspondence with reality. Postmodern cognitive nihilism was of little or no interest
to Henry because it makes adjudication of competing truth
claims and systems of truth impossible. A second universal axiom of all rational discourse about ultimate matters is that axioms (presuppositions, first principles), though unprovable, can
be tested by the criteria of logical consistency and explanatory
power. That is, those axioms are true that give rise to a coherent
system of thought and explain reality comprehensively. Finally,
according to Henry, "Propositional expressibility is, of course,
a precondition for evaluating any system. A system that is not
propositionally expressible involves no shareable truth claims
and can in no way be tested."[4] Once one accepts these basic rational, epistemological, and metaphysical axioms, Henry argued, the real fun can begin. That is, which of the several or
many competing systems of belief about ultimate reality and

---

[3]Carl F. H. Henry, *Towards a Recovery of Christian Belief* (Wheaton, IL:
Crossway Books, 1990), 88.
[4]Ibid., 71.

the meaning of the whole of reality is true? Like his mentor Clark, of course, Henry believed that only Protestant Christian orthodoxy provides a universally, publicly true account of reality; all competing belief systems are so seriously flawed in terms of coherence and explanatory power that they cannot make serious claim to belief.

What are Christianity's distinctive axioms? This was an all-important question for Henry. If one begins with flawed presuppositions, the entire system of belief is bound to fail. This is why Christianity is waning in public acceptance, Henry maintained. Its proper starting points have been replaced with faulty ones. According to Henry, the dean of evangelical theologians, there are two and only two necessary basic axioms of Christian theology, and any departure from them gives rise to something other than a truly Christian belief system and form of life: (1) the basic Christian ontological axiom of *the living God*, and (2) the basic Christian epistemological axiom of *divine revelation*. Thus, proper Christian theology—"biblical theism"—must start with *the God who speaks and shows*. Because his theology's first principles are so crucial to its entire outcome, Henry spent most of his time and energy as a theologian exploring and defending them. He became convinced early in his career as the new Evangelicalism's premier theologian that it would fail as a force for reform of both church and culture if it did not adhere strictly to these two axioms; it would inevitably fall into incoherence, subjectivism, irrelevance. The first axiom must be understood as presupposing that the God of Christianity actually exists as a transcendent-immanent person who actually communicates in a reasonable way with human beings. The second axiom must be understood as presupposing that God's revelation is "a mental activity." That is, it aims to communicate univocal (not equivocal or even analogical) truths—literal facts in propositional form—to human minds. And, of course, these divinely communicated propositions must be coherent with each other and must illumine reality and human experience of reality better than any other system of belief. Henry believed that they do and that this fact justifies embrace of Christian theology's basic presuppositions.

Besides expounding proper theological methodology (in the style of Gordon Clark), Henry expended a great deal of time and energy defending what he regarded as the classical Protestant Christian view of the Bible that has largely been abandoned by the modern churches: its nature as propositional revelation of truth; its verbal, plenary inspiration; and its inerrancy. Henry did not argue that revelation itself must necessarily be propositional or that the Bible must always be interpreted literally. He recognized and acknowledged that revelation may be personal and historical, but he argued that without propositional revelation we could not know what the "mighty acts of God" in history mean and we could not test personal revelation for accuracy. Also, the Bible contains more than direct, rational propositional communication, but without that the other literary forms of the Bible (poetry, apocalyptic imagery, etc.) would be opaque as to their meaning. *For theology*, then, according to Henry, the propositional content of the Bible is all-important. Furthermore, if the propositional content of the Bible is divine revelation and trustworthy, it must be factually reliable, supernatural communication from God and not merely the inspiring human ideas about God. Henry was careful to distinguish verbal inspiration from mechanical dictation and inerrancy from modern, technical accuracy. The point of all this, for Henry, is that Christianity is a religion of truth, not myth, and contains an irreducible doctrinal element that defines it. While Christianity is not reducible to doctrine, and faith is not reducible to rationalism, Christianity cannot live without doctrine, and faith cannot justify its beliefs without reason. Without an objective source and norm of doctrinal authority, such as only an inerrant, rational, propositional communication from God can supply, Christianity would ultimately reduce to a folk religion of subjective feelings.

Some of Henry's fellow evangelical theologians have expressed sharp disagreement with aspects of his theological method and view of divine revelation and Scripture. He has been accused of overrationalizing Christianity and of inflating the importance of propositional revelation and inerrancy. Evangelicals who have been influenced more by Pietism than by Princeton Theology, for example, find Henry's theology one-sided in its emphasis on objectivity and fear of subjectivism. It can appear overly rational and cognitive at times, and Henry's view of divine revelation may seem to imply that all the nonpropositional forms of revelation are unimportant compared with propositional revelation. Some critics believe that Henry has overreacted to neo-orthodoxy and failed to move far enough from fundamentalism. However, Henry's impact on postfundamentalist, conservative evangelical theology has been both deep and broad. His theological approach (as distinct from every specific conclusion he has reached) is the "gold standard" by which other evangelical approaches to theology tend to be judged.

12

E. J. Carnell
Apologist for Evangelical Theology

Less well known than Henry, but also influential in postfundamentalist evangelical theology is Henry's Fuller Theological Seminary colleague E. J. Carnell (1919–67). Carnell's theological career and his theological methodology both parallel Henry's rather closely. Like Henry, Carnell attended Wheaton College and came under the influence of Gordon Clark, whose rigorously rationalist methodology stamped Carnell's work as much as it did Henry's. Carnell attended Westminster Theological Seminary, founded by J. Gresham Machen, and was strongly influenced toward Calvinism there. He followed Henry at Boston University, where he pursued a doctorate in philosophy of religion and wrote a dissertation on the Danish existentialist philosopher Søren Kierkegaard under E. S. Brightman. Carnell also completed a doctorate in theology at Harvard Divinity School, where he wrote a dissertation on theologian and ethicist Reinhold Niebuhr. He taught part-time at Gordon College and helped Ockenga and Henry found Fuller Theological Seminary in Pasadena, California. Carnell moved to Fuller Theological Seminary after completing his doctoral program at Boston University. His first book, *An Introduction to Christian Apologetics*, published in 1948, won an award from its publisher, which helped propel the author into the spotlight of evangelical theology.

In 1954, at age thirty-five, much to the chagrin of some of his colleagues, Carnell succeeded Ockenga as president of Fuller Theological Seminary. Throughout the 1950s and into the 1960s the evangelical theologian and president of Evangelicalism's flagship seminary pursued an ambitious schedule of publishing, administration, teaching, and speaking. He resigned the presidency of the seminary in 1959 and suffered an emotional collapse shortly afterwards. He died of an overdose of sleeping medicine in 1968; whether his death was accidental or a suicide is unknown.

Carnell's greatest influence as an evangelical theologian came through his teaching of hundreds, if not thousands, of evangelical students at Fuller Theological Seminary during his twenty-year tenure there and through his books, which included *A Philosophy of the Christian Religion* (1952), *Christian Commitment* (1957), and *The Case for Orthodoxy* (1959). Like Henry's, Carnell's theology carried forward the rationalist philosophy of Gordon Clark by arguing in a variety of ways that sharp use of the law of noncontradiction shows that Christianity is the only truly coherent and comprehensive, systematic and rational account of the world and human life in it. He was less interested than Henry in developing a sustained polemical defense of the supernatural nature of Scripture or the propositional nature of divine revelation, although he agreed with both points. Instead, Carnell's main interests and contributions lay in demonstrating the superiority of orthodox Christianity (as defined, for example, by Augustine in the early church and

Calvin in the Reformation) over naturalism and idealist humanism and showing that liberal theology—including American neo-orthodoxy—falls short of internal consistency and explanatory power.

Much to his own chagrin and his colleagues', however, Carnell's most significant splash in the water of mid-twentieth-century theology came with the publication of *The Case for Orthodox Theology*, which was one of three volumes dedicated to the three main types of mid-century Protestant theology—liberal, neo-orthodox, and conservative. Carnell preferred "orthodox" to "conservative," just as another author, William Hordern, preferred "new Reformation theology" to "neo-orthodox theology." In his *Case* book Carnell attacked fundamentalism, much to the surprise and dismay of some of his friends and colleagues. It seemed like a waste of his scholarly energies, and his criticism seemed at times too polemical, as when he referred to fundamentalism as "orthodoxy gone cultic."[1] Overall and in general, however, Carnell's *Case* book did Evangelicalism a service by driving a second nail in the coffin of its connection with the old militant, separatistic fundamentalism. In hindsight it seems this was necessary, as many postfundamentalist evangelicals had not yet shaken off their fundamentalist past and most nonevangelicals still equated Evangelicalism with fundamentalism. In *The Case for Orthodox Theology* Carnell made clear that, at least in his view, evangelical theology is nothing more or less than contemporary historic, classical Protestant theology and not at all tied to a narrow, sectarian, dogmatic, or anti-intellectual mind-set. In the book Carnell explained the difference between Evangelicalism and fundamentalism in a way that is still used by many evangelicals:

---

[1]Edward John Carnell, *The Case for Orthodox Theology* (Philadelphia: Westminster Press, 1959), 113.

The mentality of Fundamentalism [in contrast to Evangelicalism] is dominated by ideological thinking. Ideological thinking is rigid, intolerant, and doctrinaire; it sees principles everywhere, and all principles come in clear tones of black and white; it exempts itself from the limits that original sin places on history; it wages holy wars without acknowledging the elements of pride and personal interest that prompt the call to battle; it creates new evils while trying to correct old ones.[2]

Orthodox theology—evangelical theology—is different. According to Carnell it rises above ideology and militancy, while holding fast to original Christianity against the acids of modernity and liberalism. He defined it as "that branch of Christendom which limits the ground of religious authority to the Bible"[3] without falling into literalism, separatism, intellectual stagnation, and a negative ethic. Carnell called orthodox Christianity, by which he meant Evangelicalism, away from fundamentalist habits and into the light of a better day by calling it to return to early Christianity's creeds, Reformation confessions, recognition that "all truth is God's truth," and fearless pursuit of truth using universal canons of rationality (viz., logic). Above all, he called for evangelical engagement with modern knowledge, which he sharply distinguished from intellectual trends, theories, and fashions.

---

[2]Ibid., 114.
[3]Ibid., 139.

13

Bernard Ramm
Moderate Evangelical Theologian

A third significant and influential postfundamentalist evangelical theologian was Bernard Ramm, born the same year as Carnell. His career and theology went in a somewhat different direction from either Henry's or Carnell's. Ramm was born and raised in Montana and, after a conversion experience and graduation from university, pursued seminary studies at Eastern Baptist Theological Seminary in Philadelphia and then graduate studies in philosophy at the University of Southern California, where he earned the Ph.D. in 1950. He began his teaching career at fundamentalist Los Angeles Baptist Theological Seminary and Bible Institute of Los Angeles (now Biola University). During his career as a professor of theology Ramm taught at a number of institutions, including Baylor University, Bethel College and Seminary, Eastern Baptist Theological Seminary, and American Baptist Seminary of the West. Among his most influential books are *The Christian View of Science and Scripture* (1954),

Special Revelation and the Word of God (1961), and *The Evangelical Heritage* (1973). He also wrote books on Christian apologetics (including philosophy of religion), biblical interpretation, the doctrine of sin, and Christology. Ramm was also a frequent contributor to two evangelical periodicals—*Christianity Today* and *Eternity*—and a regular speaker at Young Life summer retreats.

Like Henry and Carnell, Ramm was intent on distancing the new evangelical theology from fundamentalism, while at the same time preserving and strengthening Evangelicalism's conservative Protestant integrity over against liberal theology. His *The Evangelical Heritage* strove to demonstrate that evangelical theology and spirituality are not sectarian or modernist but instead rooted in the Protestant Reformation. Throughout his career as an evangelical theologian Ramm's primary nemesis was obscurantism—the tendency of many conservative Protestants and especially of fundamentalists to bury their heads in the sands of traditional responses to difficult questions and issues and ignore the modern world. At the same time, he did not want to throw the baby of orthodox theology out with the bathwater of obscurantism. It seems that all of the first-generation postfundamentalist evangelical theologians had to publish at least one book critical of fundamentalism to prove that they had departed decisively from it. Henry's was *The Uneasy Concience.* Carnell's was *The Case for Orthodox Theology.* Ramm's was *The Christian View of Science and Scripture,* in which he argued against those conservative Christian responses to modern science that simply ignore mountains of evidence and plain facts in favor of traditional readings of Genesis. In the book Ramm urged his evangelical readers to come to terms with modern science without capitulating to naturalistic philosophies disguised as science, and he chided fundamentalists for their attitude of "maximal conservatism." Ramm explicated a number of possible orthodox interpretations of the biblical creation narratives and promoted one, called "progressive creationism," that attempts to combine some elements of evolution with intelligent design of the universe. What had not been particularly controversial nearly a century earlier, when proposed (in rough form) by Warfield and other conservative evangelicals who wanted to correlate Scripture with the new scientific knowledge about the age of the earth, was very controversial in Ramm's time. Fundamentalists reacted angrily to Ramm's "compromise" with "godless evolution," while many younger evangelicals gladly embraced his integrative vision.

In *Special Revelation and the Word of God* Ramm tackled the difficult problem of authority for Christian belief, especially the natures of special revelation and the Bible. Rather than rooting Christian authority in the Bible per se, the author elevated the category of divine revelation above inspiration and especially above the propositions of Scripture. Divine revelation is God's self-communication in a variety of "modalities" such as historical event, incarnation, prophetic speech, and divine condescension. Scripture is one of revelation's primary "products" and takes the form of divinely inspired literature that is also, of course, accommodated to human culture, as is every modality of divine revelation. Ramm expressed caution toward extremes of "biblicism" and "criticism" within modern theology with regard to the Bible:

> The literary character of special revelation suggests another very important matter for the proper understanding of Scripture. If the Scriptures are fundamentally in the form of literature (and also of history), then they must be judged and assessed by the standards and judgments of literature, not by rules or principles foreign to them. At this point *biblicism* and *criticism* can fail to come into proper focus. Biblicism may fail to see the literary character of Scripture and treat Scripture like a code book of theological ordinances. Criticism may be so pre-

occupied with the literary aspects of Scripture that it fails to see the substance of which literature happens to be the vehicle.[1]

Ramm's criticism of biblicism may be taken as a subtle correction to Henry's and Carnell's treatments of Scripture, which place rational propositions to the fore and treat Scripture like a set of yet-to-be-systematized metaphysical and doctrinal facts. On the other hand, Ramm was critical of liberal theology and neo-orthodoxy insofar as they failed to do justice to the propositional content of the Bible as a deposit or product of divine speech. Ramm sought a balanced view of the Bible:

> The disjunction presented so frequently in modern theology between revelation as either "information" or "encounter" is false. The historic version of revelation is frequently misrepresented as if it were merely a revelation of information. Such a view is not difficult to run through with a sword. But on the other hand to represent revelation as only encounter or as only event is also defective. A professed knowledge of God which is not rooted in historical event at the critical junctures is but powerless abstraction; and historical events without a powerful interpreting word of God are opaque occurrences. The structure of special revelation calls for a hard event and a hard word of interpretation. There cannot be a hard event with a soft interpretation.[2]

Without ever denying a propositional side to divine revelation and without ever denying supernatural inspiration and infallibility of Scripture (in fact Ramm affirmed all of that!), Ramm called for evangelicals to avoid a view of revelation, in-

---

[1]Bernard Ramm, *Special Revelation and the Word of God* (Grand Rapids: Wm. B. Eerdmans, 1961), 68.
[2]Ibid., 158.

spiration, and Scripture that conflicted with the plain facts of the Bible and indulged in overrationalization for the sake of some elusive Enlightenment-like certainty. Ramm distinguished between "certitude" (assurance, confidence) and "certainty" and argued that the Holy Spirit provides the "full spiritual certitude" necessary for robust proclamation of the gospel. Rational certainty, however, is a chimera wrongly promoted by the Enlightenment and too often chased by conservative apologists. Much to the dismay of many more conservative evangelicals, Ramm rejected rational presuppositionalism and the test of coherence as the supreme test of all truth and affirmed a pattern of authority for evangelical theology that included both Word and Spirit. The ultimate guarantee of truth is not some a priori foundation, whether logic or the Bible or both; it is God himself in Jesus Christ and the Holy Spirit. The Bible is the book of Jesus Christ, and the Holy Spirit is the one who inspires and illumines the book, pointing to Jesus Christ more than to some coherent worldview. Ramm insisted on placing revelation as God's speech over inspiration, and he viewed inspiration as a dynamic process that involved the personalities of the human authors. He also relegated inerrancy to a lower place in the hierarchy of evangelical doctrines, arguing that in order to make the concept fit the plain facts of the biblical text ("phenomena of Scripture") it had to be qualified and relativized. He eschewed heated debates about inerrancy within Evangelicalism, as these, he believed, detract from the more important quality of Scripture, which is to bring humans into encounter with God through Jesus Christ.

Toward the end of his life (Ramm died in 1992), the progressive evangelical theologian began to recommend the theological method of Karl Barth—not "neo-orthodoxy"—to evangelicals. In a poorly titled book, *After Fundamentalism* (1983), Ramm dispelled many common fundamentalist and conservative evangelical myths about the great Swiss theologian—with whom Ramm studied briefly in the 1950s—and argued that Barth's theological methodology of "Christocentrism" could help evangelicals out of their obsessive love-hate relationship with the Enlightenment. According to Ramm, Barth's theology was constructed in full view of the Enlightenment without accommodating to its secularist impulses. Evangelicals could learn from Barth to be fearless with regard to all genuine questions raised by the worlds of science and philosophy—including biblical criticism—because Christianity is based on the gospel of Jesus Christ and not on some rigidly defined system of doctrines about the nature of Scripture or the way the world works. By no means did Ramm sacrifice his evangelical commitment to the authority of the Bible as God's Word, but he relativized the defensive doctrines about it—such as verbal inspiration and factual inerrancy—making them secondary to commitment to Jesus Christ and more flexible.

What is interesting is that by near the end of his life and career as a leading evangelical theologian Ramm was coming to quite the opposite conclusion regarding Barth from Henry's. Whereas Henry never gave up accusing Barth of anti-intellectualism, Ramm came to recommend Barth as the liberator of Evangelicalism from its anti-intellectual, fundamentalist roots. Ramm saw that such doctrines as biblical inerrancy, defined factually rather than functionally and separated from the gospel and the Holy Spirit, were obstacles to evangelical reform. They served only to keep evangelical theology in its fundamentalist intellectual ghetto. For Ramm, only Barth could help evangelical theology break out of that ghetto by fearlessly coming to terms with the undeniable facts of the new knowledge brought about by the Enlightenment without compromising its commitment to the gospel of free grace through Jesus Christ.

Some critics charged Ramm with capitulation to neo-orthodoxy, but the charge misses the mark. The increasingly post-conservative evangelical theologian never did deny propositional revelation or affirm that the Bible "becomes God's Word." (Whether Barth really embraced these stereotypes of neo-orthodox theology is another question worth considering!) He never rejected supernatural inspiration or every definition of inerrancy. He did, however, breathe new life into these concepts by tying them inextricably to the Holy Spirit's witness and to their main purpose of testifying to Jesus Christ and bringing people into saving encounter with him. Ramm came to see evangelical theology less as a defensive fortress against the acids of modernity and more as a second-order, flexible witness and therefore servant to divine revelation.

A nonevangelical commentator on evangelical theology, Gary Dorrien, captured the essence of Ramm's revolution in evangelical theology, which was carried on after Ramm's death by a diverse collection of postconservative evangelical thinkers. Writing with irony, Dorrien expressed Ramm's complaint and that of his postconservative disciples:

> Evangelicals are prone to fret that everything will be lost if they have no ground of absolute certainty or no proof that Christianity is superior to Islam or Buddhism. This fear drives them to impose impossible tests on Christian belief. Inerrancy or the abyss! It also drives them to invest religious authority in a posited epistemological capacity that exists outside the circle of Christian faith. The truth of Christianity is then judged by rational tests that are not only external to Christian revelation but given authority over revelation.[3]

Naturally, evangelical theologians sprung from the mold of Gordon Clark and Carl Henry (to say nothing of fundamentalists!) are critical of Ramm's and the postconservative evangeli-

---

[3]Gary Dorrien, *The Remaking of Evangelical Theology* (Louisville, KY: Westminster John Knox Press, 1998), 201.

cals' turn away from rational presuppositionalism, deductive propositionalism, verbal plenary inspiration, and strict, technical inerrancy of Scripture. To them this can only mean a reduction of the evangelical witness toward subjectivism. To postconservative evangelicals inspired by the later Ramm, however, the discovery of the epistemological role of the Holy Spirit, embrace of paradoxes, abandonment of a defensive, often hostile attitude toward the Enlightenment and culture, and willingness to reconsider traditional evangelical notions of inspiration and inerrancy have the same exhilarating feel experienced by the postfundamentalist evangelicals in the 1940s and 1950s as they took the risk of stepping outside the stifling abode of fundamentalism. The harsh criticisms of their conservative evangelical colleagues remind them of the hardening of the categories among the fundamentalists who condemned the neoevangelicals for opening their minds and methods to the larger world of ideas and of education.

14

Donald Bloesch
Progressive Evangelical Theologian

A fourth influential evangelical theologian closely associated with the postfundamentalist evangelical coalition is Donald G. Bloesch (b. 1928). Bloesch represents something of an anomaly, as he has never taught at a college, university, or seminary that is part of the evangelical coalition, nor was any of his theological education completed in an evangelical institution. In other words, unlike the other theologians under consideration here, Bloesch has never operated within the evangelical subculture except by publishing book reviews and articles in *Christianity Today* and *Eternity*. Some of his books have been published by evangelical publishers. Bloesch was raised in and has always remained a part of the Protestant mainstream; he was untouched by the fundamentalist movement and its militancy and separatism. Revivalism is not part of his heritage. Because of all this, he is sometimes dismissed as a "mediating theologian" rather than a true postfundamentalist evangelical thinker. Nevertheless, he has produced a large body of theological literature that is closely identified with postfundamentalist Evangelicalism, and he has stood as an influential theological voice on the boundary between mainline Protestantism and the evangelical coalition.

Bloesch's evangelical theology attempts to combine several seemingly disparate strands of Protestant thought: magisterial Protestantism with its catholicity (emphasis on the church universal throughout the ages) and confessionalism (emphasis on formal, written statements of belief), Reformed theology within a free-church framework, Pietism, and neo-orthodoxy (especially the theologies of Karl Barth and Emil Brunner). Bloesch pursued his doctoral studies in theology at the University of Chicago, where he studied with leading liberal Protestant thinkers and wrote his dissertation on the apologetics of American neo-orthodox theologian and ethicist Reinhold Niebuhr. While at the University of Chicago's Divinity School he became involved with the university's chapter of InterVarsity Christian Fellowship—a moderate evangelical student group. Bloesch's strongly Pietist early spiritual formation inclined him toward Evangelicalism more than toward the liberalism he was encountering at the Divinity School. Nevertheless, he studied liberal theology—including process theology—in order to understand it on its own terms and has remained in close dialogue with liberal Protestant thought throughout his life. After receiving his doctorate in theology, the Indiana-born young theologian went to Europe to study at Oxford and at Basel, where he met and was impressed with Barth. Upon returning to the United States, he embarked on a teaching career at the Presbyterian-related University of Dubuque Theological Seminary in Iowa, from which he retired in 1993 after thirty-five years.

Bloesch has authored between thirty-five and forty books (some are moving toward publication as this is being written), including two sets of systematic theology. Many of his books have promoted spiritual and theological renewal in the American church; some have especially focused on Evangelicalism and its renewal through rediscovering its roots in the early church and Reformation and through overcoming sectarianism and strife over secondary matters of the Christian faith. Among his most notable and influential volumes are *The Evangelical Renaissance* (1973), *The Future of Evangelical Christianity: A Call for Unity amid Diversity* (1983), *Essentials of Evangelical Theology* (2 volumes, 1978 and 1979), and a seven-volume system of theology—undoubtedly his magnum opus—with the series title Christian Foundations. Bloesch's primary contribution to evangelical thought has been to call it out of its captivity to the old liberal-fundamentalist controversy and out of narrow sectarianism and into a greater appreciation for the historic Reformation tradition with an emphasis on spirituality.

In this project, spanning more than thirty years, the Iowa theologian has stood on the shoulders of previous Protestant thinkers such as John Calvin, the Pietists Spener and Zinzendorf, John Wesley, Jonathan Edwards, the "melancholy Dane" Søren Kierkegaard, English Christian theologians P. T. Forsyth and John Stott, and twentieth-century neo-orthodox thinkers Karl Barth and Emil Brunner. Notably missing from the list are fundamentalists, including very conservative postfundamentalist evangelicals. Bloesch has never sympathized with or wished to promote rationalism, including evangelical presuppositionalism and propositionalism (Henry, Carnell, et al.). Also notably missing, however, are liberals. While engaging in constructive dialogue with liberal Protestant theologians, Bloesch has never viewed himself or his theology as a version of liberal thought or sympathetic with it. He prefers to describe himself as a "progressive evangelical" and a "catholic evangelical theologian." These two labels point to twin concerns of Bloesch's theology: to retrieve the great tradition of Christian theology, especially as that was reformed and renewed by the sixteenth-century Protestant reformers, and to keep evangelical theology both faithful to its roots and reforming itself in light of new knowledge and "new light" breaking forth from God's Word. In *Essentials of Evangelical Theology* Bloesch clearly set forth his centrist evangelical theological intention: "The theological options today are liberalism or modernism . . . , a reactionary Evangelicalism or Fundamentalism, and a catholic Evangelicalism, which alone is truly evangelical and biblical."[1]

Bloesch labels his theological method "fideistic revelationism," which requires a bit of explaining. This approach to constructive Christian theology avoids the extremes of both rationalism and sheer fideism (blind faith) while combining faith and reason in the service of God's Word, which stands over them:

> While rationalism holds to *credo quia intelligo* (I believe because I understand) and fideism to *credo quia absurdum est* (I believe because it is absurd), evangelical theology in the classical tradition subscribes to *credo ut intelligam* (I believe in order to understand). In this last view faith is neither a blind leap into the unknown (Kierkegaard) nor an assent of the will to what reason has already shown to be true (Carl Henry), but a venture of trust based on evidence that faith itself provides. We do not believe without our reason, but we also do not believe on the basis of reason. Faith entails thinking and examining. In order to come to a mature faith we need to search and examine the Scriptures as well as the tradition of the church.[2]

[1]Donald G. Bloesch, *Essentials of Evangelical Theology*, vol. 2: *Life, Ministry, and Hope* (San Francisco: Harper & Row, 1979), 283.

[2]Donald G. Bloesch, *A Theology of Word and Spirit: Authority and Method in Theology*, Christian Foundations, vol. 1 (Downers Grove, IL: InterVarsity Press, 1992), 58. For a critical analysis of Bloesch's theological

Bloesch seeks to guide theological reflection and construction between two dangerous rocks: the Scylla of experientialism and the Charybdis of philosophism. Experientialism allows the individual's subjective feelings to guide and control Christian belief and confession. In a more sophisticated form it appears in the theology of Schleiermacher, according to Bloesch, as the religious a priori of universal human God-consciousness. In either case, it shipwrecks Christianity and theology on the rock of subjectivism. Just as great a danger, however, is philosophism, which in the form of rationalism shipwrecks theology by giving control to autonomous (unregenerate) human intellect and, inevitably, some particular philosophical school of thought. According to Bloesch this danger appears whenever Christian theologians begin their reflections with some presupposed system of philosophical thought or a priori rules of reason, rather than with God's Word—special divine revelation. Instead, he avers, authentic Christian theology must always use reason in the service of revelation and must remain suspicious of philosophical systems that threaten to predetermine what God's Word can say and what it can mean.

For Bloesch, the renewal of Evangelicalism requires rejection of rationalistic, apologetic approaches to theology and retrieval of the Reformation method of Word and Spirit, in which all authority—even authenticating authority—rests in the Holy Spirit-attested Word of God, which creates faith rather than being authenticated by human faith:

Against [rationalism] I contend that the claims of Christianity are true because they rest on events that really happened, events that cannot possibly be synchronized

method, see Stanley J. Grenz, "'Fideistic Revelationism': Donald Bloesch's Antirationalist Theological Method," in *Evangelical Theology in Transition: Theologians in Dialogue with Donald Bloesch*, ed. Elmer M. Colyer (Downers Grove, IL: InterVarsity Press, 1999), 35-60.

or harmonized with ordinary human experience and reason; and because their credibility and veracity is confirmed in our hearts by the Spirit of God himself as he authenticates the message of faith in the church through the ages where the Bible is read and believed and where the faith is proclaimed in fidelity and love. Because human reason is in the service of sin apart from faith (Rom. 8:7, 14:23), it needs to be shattered and transformed before it can lay hold of the mystery of the truth of the gospel, which is hidden from natural sight and understanding but becomes the glorious possession of those who break with the arrogance and pretension that presently cloud their reasoning and cry out for salvation that God alone can and does provide in the person of his Son, Jesus Christ.[3]

Thus, Bloesch's theology is intended to be a "kerygmatic theology" rather than an "apologetic theology," and it is self-consciously set against the rationalistic approaches to evangelical theology that dominated the early postfundamentalist evangelical coalition's beginnings (Clark, Henry, Carnell). It is most closely comparable with the neo-orthodox or dialectical theologies of Barth and Emil Brunner. However, Bloesch is not satisfied with neo-orthodoxy's doctrine of Scripture and with some of Barth's or Brunner's specific ideas. While expressing genuine regard for Barth's theology, Bloesch criticizes the Swiss theologian's doctrine of salvation in *Jesus Is Victor!: Karl Barth's Doctrine of Salvation* (1976). Sprinkled throughout his books are numerous positive references to both Barth and Brunner. He shares enthusiastically their rejections of natural knowledge of God and literalistic biblicism (Brunner's accusation that some conservative Protestants have exchanged a pope in Rome for a "paper pope"). On the other hand, he is always

---

[3]Ibid., 272.

careful to distance himself from their criticisms of belief in the inspiration and infallibility of Scripture. Bloesch's preferred term for his own view of the relationship between divine revelation (God's Word) and Scripture is "sacramental." Once again, this is intended to mediate between distorted and extreme views. Against liberal Protestant theology Bloesch argues for a close relationship between the Bible and supernatural divine revelation; against Fundamentalism he argues for a distinction between them. "The Bible is not in and of itself the revelation of God but the divinely appointed means and channel of this revelation. . . . The Word of God transcends the human witness, and yet it comes to us only in the servant form of the human words."[4]

Bloesch breaks decisively with fundamentalism and the rationalist-propositionalist view of revelation when he illustrates his sacramental view:

> One might say that the Bible is the Word of God in a formal sense—as a light bulb is related to light. The light bulb is not itself the light but its medium. The light of God's truth is ordinarily shining in the Bible, but it is discerned only by the eyes of faith. Even Christians, however, do not see the light in its full splendor. It is refracted and obscured by the form of the Bible, but it nonetheless reaches us if we have faith.[5]

Bloesch makes clear that he holds a high view of Scripture as God's inspired witness to Jesus Christ, who is God's Word in person. The Holy Spirit communicates Jesus Christ and spiritual truth and life through the Bible as through no other earthly medium (aside from Jesus' humanity). And yet, Bloesch

---

[4]Donald G. Bloesch, *Holy Scripture: Revelation, Inspiration and Interpretation,* Christian Foundations, vol. 2 (Downers Grove, IL: InterVarsity Press, 1994), 57.
[5]Ibid., 59.

avers, even the Bible has its "highs" and "lows," in that "the message of revelation is explicit in some parts of the Bible and implicit in others" and the Bible contains flaws and blemishes that remind us of its "participation in the real world of decay and death."[6] Bloesch drives the nail in the coffin of a fundamentalist view of Scripture (so far as he is concerned) when he affirms that "our final authority [for Christian faith and practice] is not what the Bible says but what God says in the Bible."[7] Ultimately, it is the task of the Spirit-guided exegete of Scripture to discern the difference.

Bloesch holds to a high view of Scripture—even if some conservative evangelicals do not think so. "I hold to an ontic difference between the Bible and other books, for the Bible has both a divine origin and a divine goal."[8] He makes abundantly clear that he regards the Bible as unique in its authority for Christian faith and practice in that it stands in judgment over all traditions and thoughts of human beings. He affirms the classical Protestant *sola scriptura* and argues that the Bible is supernaturally inspired by the Holy Spirit of God and is the indispensable witness to Jesus Christ. On the other hand, he questions traditional evangelical interpretations of both inspiration of Scripture and of Scripture's inerrancy. With Baptist theologian Strong a century earlier, Bloesch affirms a dynamic rather than a verbal view of inspiration: "In my view inspiration is the divine election and superintendence of particular writers and writings in order to ensure a trustworthy and potent witness to the truth."[9] As for verbal inspiration, "It means that the words of human beings [the authors of Scripture] are adopted [by the Holy Spirit] to serve the purposes of God."[10]

---

[6]Ibid.
[7]Ibid., 60.
[8]Ibid., 128.
[9]Ibid., 119.
[10]Ibid., 120.

Without denying a propositional aspect to revelation in Scripture, Bloesch states that the "purpose of inspiration is not the production of an errorless book but the regeneration of the seeker after truth."[11] As for inerrancy, "[a] distinction should always be made between what Scripture reports and includes and what it teaches or intends."[12] In other words, the Bible is without error in matters crucial to the encounter with God and salvation but not in every detail: "Scriptural inerrancy can be affirmed if it means the conformity of what is written to the dictates of the Spirit regarding the will and purpose of God. But it cannot be held if it is taken to mean the conformity of everything that is written in Scripture to the facts of world history and science."[13] Bloesch prefers the term "infallible" to "inerrant" for describing Scripture's trustworthiness.

Bloesch's theology creates a hybrid between the strict propositionalism and rationalism of the first generation of postfundamentalist evangelical theologians (Henry, Carnell, et al.) and neo-orthodoxy (Barth, Brunner). However, it is much closer to the classical evangelical synthesis of Protestant orthodoxy and Pietism than to either fundamentalism or neo-orthodoxy, and there is nothing liberal about it (except its liberality as displayed in its generous orthodoxy). Bloesch's influence within Evangelicalism has been a moderating one that helps postfundamentalists discover on a number of crucial theological matters a centrist view that is not mediocre or lukewarm. His is a strongly confessional Protestant theology that affirms all the classical doctrines of Christian orthodoxy stripped of their sectarian imbalance introduced by fundamentalism and often maintained by conservative evangelicals. Conservative evangelicals often find Bloesch frustrating; he is notoriously diffi-

---

[11]Ibid., 118.
[12]Ibid., 127-28.
[13]Ibid., 107.

cult to categorize. He is certainly not modernist or liberal. His critiques of liberal and radical theologies are devastating, and yet he finds something of value in almost every theologian. His treatment of the controversial issues of feminism, patriarchy, and inclusive language for God is a good example of his non-liberal, mediating approach. While affirming equality of women with men in every area of life, Bloesch condemns radical revisioning of God (e.g., as "divine Mother") and calls instead for retrieval of biblical feminine metaphors for God. He is certainly not fundamentalist or even traditionally conservative as an evangelical. He consistently criticizes Carl Henry and that type of evangelical rationalism and propositionalism as wooden and sterile. And yet he affirms the supernatural reality of God and God's activity, efficacy of prayer, miracles and classical orthodox doctrines.

What Bloesch brings to Evangelicalism is a balanced perspective that is free from the distorting effects of fundamentalism and the internecine battles that have racked Evangelicalism because of its fundamentalist roots. Yet his influence within Evangelicalism is somewhat muted because he is widely regarded as a "mainliner"—a theologian who may be relatively conservative theologically (in the overall scheme of things) but stands outside the evangelical subculture ("Evangelicalism") and speaks more *to* it than *from within* it. To the extent this is true, however, it may just be the reason he is able to speak such a moderating, balanced message that many, if not most, evangelical theologians need to hear and heed.

15

Postconservative
Evangelical Theology

At the turn of the century and millennium, evangelical theology is undergoing special stress and strain. Up until this time, most evangelical theologians have been *postfundamentalist* and yet *conservative*. Postfundamentalist evangelical theology during the first half-century of its existence has been marked by a profound anxiety of wanting to distance itself from fundamentalism without being anything other than conservative or traditional. Fear of theological liberalism and fundamentalism has been its obsession. As soon as someone moves too far from fundamentalism—even in terms of harsh rhetoric against its narrowness and dogmatism—he or she falls under "concern" by fellow evangelicals for possibly moving too close to liberalism. The same thing happens whenever an evangelical calls for dialogue with liberals in theology. Anyone who talks of separation from heretical or apostate denominations falls under suspicion from some quarters of having a fundamentalist spirit.

In this milieu of evangelical obsessiveness over its own

identity vis-à-vis liberalism and fundamentalism, a few coura-
geous evangelical thinkers have begun to step out and develop
what can best be described as a *postconservative* evangelical theology.[1] Postconservative does not indicate "anti-conservative"
(contrary to what some critics have suggested) but only a desire
to move beyond the category of conservatism insofar as it bi-
ases Evangelicalism and evangelical theology in favor of the
status quo and keeps it bound to its fundamentalist heritage
and habits. Postconservative evangelicals are extremely diverse
and can hardly be called a movement. They represent a mood
that is dissatisfied with old forms of old debates and with tradi-
tionalism for its own sake and especially with maximal conservatism. They believe that "the received evangelical tradition"
(whatever that is, exactly) is often a form of bondage that hin-
ders creativity, innovation, and renewal. There is no organization of postconservative evangelicals; they prefer to network
with each other and with nonevangelicals. By and large they
consider the Evangelical Theological Society too narrow and
restrictive; they do not like its requirement of belief in and confession of inerrancy for membership. Postconservatives tend to
think "outside the box" and are willing to take risks in reforming traditional evangelical formulas. They think of theology as
a journey or pilgrimage and of theologians as pioneers rather
than guardians or gatekeepers. They desire a "generous orthodoxy" that eschews both narrow dogmatism and liberal relativism. They see value in constructive evangelical engagement
and dialogue with postmodern culture and philosophy and are

---

[1]For description and critique of this new movement (or mood) among
evangelical theologians, see Roger E. Olson, "Postconservative Evangelicals Greet the Postmodern Age," *Christian Century,* 112, no. 15
(May 3, 1995): 480-83; Gary Dorrien, *The Remaking of Evangelical Theology* (Louisville, KY: Westminster John Knox Press, 1998); and Millard Erickson, *The Evangelical Left: Encountering Postconservative Evangelical Theology* (Grand Rapids: Baker Books, 1997).

saddened by the harsh polemics that evangelicals often hurl at nonevangelicals and secular culture. Above all, postconservative evangelicals want to rise above the traditional spectrum of "left" (liberal) and "right" (conservative) in modern theology by leaving behind obsessions with issues of the Enlightenment and liberal or fundamentalist habits of the mind.[2] They are willing to reconsider traditional evangelical doctrinal formulations insofar as they are held only because they are traditional and defensive against liberal theology.

The acknowledged leader of postconservative evangelical theology is maverick Canadian evangelical theologian Clark Pinnock (b. 1937). While he is certainly not formally the leader of postconservative evangelical theologians and has not identified himself that way, he is the best known and most widely discussed and influential theologian of this new evangelical theological mood.[3] By his own confession, Pinnock's early evangelical journey was quite typical. He was raised in a fairly liberal Baptist church in Ontario, Canada, but his grandparents were deeply pious, evangelical missionaries to Africa. Their influence on his life was more profound than he realized as a child and young person. In 1950 he experienced conversion to Christ and, by his own confession, became a fundamentalist. His spiritual and theological life was being nurtured and shaped by radio preachers such as Charles Fuller, Billy Graham, and Donald Grey Barnhouse. He became involved with the Youth for Christ movement in Toronto and there also fell under the influence of famous fundamentalist pastor Oswald J. Smith, pastor of the Peoples Church. Later he was influenced

---

[2]See Nancey Murphy, *Beyond Liberalism and Fundamentalism: How Moderns and Postmodern Philosophy Set the Theological Agenda* (Valley Forge, PA: Trinity Press International, 1996).

[3]See the intellectual biography of Pinnock by Barry L. Callen, *Clark Pinnock: Journey Toward Renewal* (Nappanee, IN: Evangel Publishing House, 2000).

by the Keswick movement, InterVarsity Christian Fellowship, Francis Schaeffer's L'Abri retreat and movement, and by Christian authors such as C. S. Lewis and John R. Stott. After graduating from university in Canada, Pinnock began doctoral studies in New Testament with British evangelical scholar F. F. Bruce at the University of Manchester in England.

After completing his doctoral work, the young evangelical scholar returned to North America and taught at a succession of seminaries: New Orleans Baptist Theological Seminary, Trinity Evangelical Divinity School, Regent College, and McMaster Divinity College. His major works include *A Defense of Biblical Infallibility* (1967), *Reason Enough: A Case for the Christian Faith* (1980), *The Scripture Principle* (1985), *A Wideness in God's Mercy* (1992), *Flame of Love: A Theology of the Holy Spirit* (1996), and *Most Moved Mover: A Theology of the Openness of God* (2001). Pinnock also edited several volumes, contributed to many more, and published numerous articles. His early writings reveal his early conservative, rationalistic, and Reformed orientation. Under the influence of Carl Henry and Francis Schaeffer the young Pinnock followed the traditional postfundamentalist evangelical line very closely and was aggressive in his defenses of biblical inerrancy and rationalist apologetics. He was brought from England to New Orleans by the seminary president to "hold the line" against neo-orthodoxy there. (Whether there really was an influence of neo-orthodoxy at that seminary or that was a false perception is debatable.)

In midcareer, while teaching theology at Trinity Evangelical Divinity School in suburban Chicago, Pinnock began to undergo a change in theological orientation that he described in a chapter entitled "From Augustine to Arminius: A Pilgrimage in Theology." There he stated that "I guess it is time for evangelicals to grow up and recognize that evangelical theology is not an uncontested body of timeless truth. There are various accounts of it. . . . Like it or not, we are embarked on a pilgrimage in theology and cannot determine exactly where will it [*sic*] lead and how it will end."[4] As part of his theological turn he came to understand doctrine as changeable and theology as a pilgrimage toward truth. To his critics this seemed relativistic, but to Pinnock it was merely appreciation for the theologian's own finitude and fallenness. As part of his change Pinnock turned away from the Augustinian-Calvinist model of God and God's relationship with the world (God as the all-determining reality) toward the Arminian model of God's self-limiting relationship with humanity for the sake of human freedom and participation in their own salvation. Even as he began to throw off Reformed theology, he realized that it might mean a radical revisioning of God's attributes toward a more relational understanding. Eventually he did develop and promote the idea of God's "openness"—that God freely chooses to learn what the future holds as humans use their free will to make morally responsible decisions. He has consistently argued that he came to this view independently of the liberal school of thought known as process theology and that he has little sympathy with it, but his critics have often charged him with compromising with that perceived enemy of evangelical thought.

Another change came about in Pinnock's understanding of Scripture. In *The Scripture Principle* he affirmed a high view of Scripture stripped of fundamentalist and conservative evangelical biblicism. While paying lip service to inerrancy (minimized and highly qualified), the pilgrim theologian argued for evangelical acknowledgment of diversity within the Bible:

> I suggest that we think of inspiration in broader terms than is customary—less as a punctilinear enlightenment of a few elect persons and more as a long-term divine activity operating within the whole history of revelation. In-

[4]In *The Grace of God and the Will of Man: A Case for Arminianism,* ed. Clark H. Pinnock (Grand Rapids: Zondervan, 1989), 28.

spiration means that God gave us the Scriptures, but it does not dictate how we must think of the individual units being produced. Scripture exists because of the will of God and is a result of his ultimate causality, but it comes into existence through many gifts of prophecy, insight, imagination, and wisdom that the Spirit gives as he wills. The all-important point is that everything taught in the Scriptures is meant to be heard and heeded, because it is divinely intended. Every segment is inspired by God, though not in the same way, and the result is a richly variegated teacher, richer for all its diversity. The very differences are what enables the Bible to speak with power and relevance to so many different people in so many different settings, and to address the many-sidedness of the human condition.[5]

As Pinnock continued on his journey in theology he reconsidered the issue of salvation and discovered a "wideness in God's mercy" that stops short of universal salvation but requires embrace of "inclusivism." In *A Wideness in God's Mercy: The Finality of Jesus Christ in a World of Religions,* the maverick evangelical theologian threw out the traditional evangelical pessimism about the possibility of salvation for the unevangelized and argued in favor of an "optimism of salvation" in Christ for those who never had a chance to hear about the Savior of the world. "God sent Jesus to be the Savior of the world, not the Savior of a select few."[6] Pinnock argued from the logic of God's love and provision of redemption that any sincere truth-seeker may be encountered by God on the journey toward truth and be reconciled to God by God's grace and mercy. Contrary to

---

[5]Clark H. Pinnock, *The Scripture Principle* (San Francisco: Harper & Row, 1984), 64.
[6]Clark H. Pinnock, *A Wideness in God's Mercy: The Finality of Jesus Christ in a World of Religions* (Grand Rapids: Zondervan, 1992), 47.

critics, nowhere does Pinnock affirm unconditional universal salvation; instead he affirms that God does not automatically reject all who do not hear and explicitly respond to the gospel message as preached by a Christian missionary. In several publications he has suggested a postmortem opportunity for acceptance of Jesus Christ for the unevangelized. In *A Wideness in God's Mercy*, however, he suggests that people may be saved by Jesus Christ (never apart from his life and death) through the universal light of God that is present in human conscience and cultures.

Another part of Pinnock's postconservative theological pilgrimage is his experience with the charismatic movement and the so-called Third Wave of the Holy Spirit in the "signs and wonders movement." He became involved in a charismatic Bible study and prayer meeting in the 1970s and then in the Vineyard movement in Toronto. While retaining his Baptist identity and church membership, Pinnock began to consider himself part of the Third Wave of the Holy Spirit (the first being Pentecostalism, the second the charismatic movement) associated with the ministry of John Wimber and his followers. In *Flame of Love: A Theology of the Holy Spirit* the Canadian evangelical theologian sought to bring the person and work of the Holy Spirit back into the foreground of evangelical theological reflection without in any way diminishing the roles of the Father and the Son. There he affirmed the present supernatural activity of the Spirit in all of the gifts mentioned in the New Testament (contra traditional evangelical cessationism) while admonishing Pentecostals. With regard to speaking in tongues, he proposed the principle that while it is normal, it is not the norm. In other words, unlike conventional evangelicals who resist tongues and other supernatural gifts of utterance, Pinnock believes these are contemporary gifts of the Spirit to the churches and should be practiced by believers; but unlike classical Pentecostals and many charismatics, he does not think they are required signs of spiritual life.

Finally, Pinnock broke the patience of many conservative evangelicals by rejecting conventional theism or classical theism and embracing what he calls the "openness of God," or "open theism." Although he had strongly hinted at it earlier, Pinnock first laid out his program for a new evangelical understanding of God's relationship with the world in *The Openness of God*, which he coauthored with four other evangelical theologians and philosophers in 1994. In his chapter, entitled simply "Systematic Theology," he argued that so-called classical theism is problematic from a biblical perspective and also inconsistent with many essential aspects of evangelical Christian spirituality. For example, Scripture reveals God as interactive with humans, such that prayer can change God's mind. And yet classical theism and much of the received evangelical tradition claims that God is strictly immutable. Also, if prayer cannot change God's mind because God is strictly immutable, why pray petitionary prayers at all? If God already foreknows the future exhaustively and infallibly, there does not seem to be any urgency in petitionary prayers such as evangelicals traditionally pray. In *The Openness of God* and in his later volume, *Most Moved Mover* (2001), Pinnock laid out an entire program for the renewal of evangelical theism through an infusion of "biblical theism." God, he argues, voluntarily limits himself such that he can be affected by the free-will decisions and prayers of his human creatures. Futhermore, God does not know the future exhaustively and infallibly, because much of the future is determined by genuinely free decisions of human beings, and God will not abrogate that freedom by determining all decisions and actions—which would be the only way God could foreknow them. For Pinnock and other open theists (Gregory Boyd, John Sanders, et al.) this is the only view that does justice to God's personal interaction with human beings in history. To their critics it is heresy, if not idolatry. The controversy surrounding open theism led to a resolution by the Evangelical Theological Society in 2001 affirming God's absolute knowledge of all events past, present, and future.

Pinnock has been and remains both a catalyst for reform and renewal and a lightning rod for controversy within Evangelicalism and among evangelical theologians. He has been called a pioneer, a moving target, and a false prophet. Few who know his theology are indifferent to it. His overall impact on evangelical theology remains to be seen; his career is not completed and his magnum opus remains unwritten. He may never write a theological system or anything approaching it, because he prefers the journey model, which centers around ad hoc contributions to theology, to the closed system model, which seeks to summarize all theological truth in a coherent system. Although Pinnock has not explicitly embraced postmodernism, it seems that he is influenced by postmodernity, whether he is aware of that or not. He has expressed strong sympathy for narrative theology that views divine revelation more as story (epic, not fiction) than as a set of propositions and called for a "postmodern orthodoxy."[7] For him, then, the "essence of Christianity" is the "epic story of salvation," rather than law, dogma, theory, or experience. Doctrine is second-order speech that seeks to interpret the metanarrative delivered in Scripture. Systematic theology, Pinnock fears, tends to replace the narrative structure of revelation with all its wonder and mystery. However, Pinnock's sympathizers hope that he will eventually write a summary of Christian doctrine from his own postconservative evangelical perspective. They find his approach refreshing and liberating as well as consistent both with the gospel of Jesus Christ and the best of postmodern culture that resists absolutiz-

---

[7]Clark H. Pinnock, *Tracking the Maze: Finding Our Way Through Modern Theology from an Evangelical Perspective* (San Francisco: Harper & Row, 1990).

ing and totalizing metanarratives.

What do these five postfundamentalist evangelical theologians have in common? What makes Carl Henry, E. J. Carnell, Bernard Ramm, Donald Bloesch, and Clark Pinnock all *"evangelical* theologians"? They do not agree about basic theological methodology; some push universal canons of reason to the fore in theology, while others reject such and elevate divine revelation and faith over reason and evidence. They do not agree about the nature of divine revelation entirely; some insist on the primacy of propositions in revelation while others promote nonpropositional aspects of revelation such as incarnation, encounter, and narrative. They do not agree about the nature of Scripture; some argue for its verbal, plenary inspiration and strict inerrancy in all matters, while others view inspiration as dynamic and prefer infallibility to inerrancy. The diversity within evangelical theology becomes even greater when one includes other evangelical theologians in the list for comparison.

What makes them all evangelical is their common commitment to a supernatural life and worldview, the Bible as the supernaturally inspired and infallible Word of God, Jesus Christ as God and Savior, the triune, transcendent-immanent God of the Bible as creator of all things, salvation through conversion to Jesus Christ by repentance and faith and through grace alone, world transformation through evangelism and social action, and the cross of Jesus Christ (i.e., his atoning death) as the only hope for and means of reconciliation and redemption of lost humanity. Compared with many other groups of Christian theologians and movements within Christian theology, then, these five and all evangelical theologians have much in common. Together they form a distinct alternative to classical Roman Catholic theology and liberal Protestant thought, as well as to all the radical and liberationist theologies of the late twentieth century. Tensions within evangelical theology and among evangelical theologians threaten to dissolve that unity, however, and if they are not careful, they will experience a balkanization of evangelical theology that will cause it to cease to exist as a relatively unified movement. The final portion of this historical essay will be a brief overview of those tensions within evangelical theology.

16

Tensions
in Evangelical
Theology

The postfundamentalist evangelical coalition was born with diversity, and yet some of its leaders—including its leading theologians—expected their own preferred theological orientations to dominate it. This is probably the most profound cause of tension within evangelical theology—the feelings of superiority and neglect among different types of evangelicals. Most of the early movers and shakers of the evangelical coalition in the 1940s and 1950s were theologically Reformed. That is, they looked back to Augustine, John Calvin, Ulrich Zwingli, Martin Bucer, and Jonathan Edwards as the great heroes of the evangelical faith. Bernard Ramm displayed this tendency to elevate Reformed theology over its alternatives in his *The Evangelical Heritage*. He almost totally ignored the contributions of non-Reformed theologians, such as the Anabaptists Balthasar Hubmaier and Menno Simons, the Pietists, John Wesley, Charles

Finney, and other Arminian and free-church theologians. Evangelical historian George Marsden has also highlighted the Reformed roots of Evangelicalism in his influential accounts of evangelical history. Many evangelical writers treat the subject as if Reformed theology is normative for Evangelicalism. All the while, of course, many evangelical lay people, pastors, and leaders, as well as influential evangelists and missionaries, are Arminian, Wesleyan, or Pentecostal. The National Association of Evangelicals includes at least as many non-Reformed member churches and denominations as Reformed ones.

In response to this bent toward Reformed thinking in evangelical theology, evangelical historian Donald Dayton has raised the argument that the "Pentecostal Paradigm" of evangelical history is just as likely and probably truer to the facts than the "Presbyterian Paradigm" of Marsden and others. The Pentecostal Paradigm refers to a view that authentic Evangelicalism and evangelical theology is revivalistic and at least implicitly Arminian, not Reformed.[1] The Presbyterian Paradigm refers to the view—opposed by Dayton but attributed to Marsden—that authentic Evangelicalism and evangelical theology is rooted in the Puritans and the Princeton School of theology. This debate and the hard feelings associated with it were raised to a new pitch of intensity with the founding of the Alliance of Confessing Evangelicals in the 1990s. Its publication, *Modern Reformation,* promotes the belief that authentic evangelical theology is indeed Reformed, or at least rooted in the Lutheran-Reformed (monergistic) Reformation and its doctrines of absolute divine sovereignty.

Tensions between conservative, aggressive Calvinist evangelicals and defensive Arminian evangelicals threaten to dis-

---

[1]See Donald W. Dayton, "The Search for the Historical Evangelicalism: George Marsden's History of Fuller Seminary as a Case Study," *Christian Scholar's Review* 23, no. 1 (September 1993).

rupt the uneasy harmony of the evangelical theological community. As long as Billy Graham is alive and well and able robustly to hold the evangelical coalition together in spite of all its diversity, these tensions remain just under the surface. Once the "Graham glue" dissolves with his retirement or death, it seems likely that at least the more dogmatic group of Reformed evangelicals and more defensive group of Arminian (including Wesleyan) evangelicals will break away from each other and disrupt the evangelical coalition.

Another tension within evangelical theology is between *reformist* and *traditionalist* evangelical theologians. Traditionalists favor a "forward to the past" program for evangelical strength. That is, they regard reform and renewal as retrieval of tradition. Thomas Oden is a Methodist evangelical theologian who was formerly liberal and taught for many years at Methodist-related Drew Theological Seminary. In several volumes and numerous articles he has called for a rediscovery of the authority of the early church's teaching as a "consensual tradition" through which Scripture must be interpreted. His three-volume *Systematic Theology* (San Francisco: Harper & Row, 1987–92) is a compendium of early Christian teaching on all the traditional doctrinal loci of theology; he argues that the consensus of the church fathers and great creeds of Christendom must function for even Protestant Christians as a "rule of faith" alongside of Scripture.

Reformists favor a "new light" program for evangelical renewal. That is, they regard truth as continually breaking forth from God's Word, correcting tradition, and reforming the church and its theology. Pinnock is a reformist, as was Stanley J. Grenz (1950-2005), who wrote numerous volumes of evangelical theology, including *Revisioning Evangelical Theology* (Downers Grove, IL: InterVarsity Press, 1993), which elevates "conversional piety" over doctrine as the essence of evangelical faith. Reformists believe that the constructive task of theology is never finished; traditionalists consider the only valid tasks of theology as instructional and critical. Traditionalists tend to be more concerned with evangelical identity and boundaries, whereas reformists are more concerned with diversity in unity through an evangelical community with a strong center but no definite boundaries. These two parties of evangelical theologians often fall into tension with each other.[2] Traditionalists tend to view reformists as soft on doctrine and relativistic with regard to truth; reformists tend to view traditionalists as dogmatic, reactionary, and irrelevant to contemporary issues and concerns facing Christians.

A third area of evangelical theological tension surrounds the nature of Scripture. Evangelical theologians have never reached complete agreement about this crucial matter. In 1977 influential evangelical theologian and editor of *Christianity Today* Harold Lindsell published a bombshell book, entitled *The Battle for the Bible* (Grand Rapids: Zondervan), that argued that belief in strict biblical inerrancy—including inerrancy in matters of history and cosmology—is an essential of evangelical faith. The book was written partly in response to an earlier work by evangelical theologian Dewey Beegle, entitled *Scripture, Tradition, and Infallibility* (Grand Rapids: Wm. B. Eerdmans, 1973), that argued that Scripture is simply not inerrant or infallible and that one can believe in its inspiration and authority without overlooking or denying its factual errors in matters unrelated to salvation. Lindsell disagreed most vehemently and identified evangelical scholars and institutions whom he considered less than authentically evangelical because they did not affirm inerrancy in the way he believed it must be affirmed. (Lindsell went so far as to posit six crowings of the rooster in the incident of Peter's denial of Jesus in order to harmonize the Gospel accounts!)

---

[2]See Roger E. Olson, "The Future of Evangelical Theology," *Christianity Today* 42, no. 2 (February 9, 1998): 40-48.

The fallout from the book was disastrous for evangelical unity. It helped propel the entire Southern Baptist Convention—America's largest Protestant denomination—into a twenty-year convulsion. Almost overnight evangelical organizations and institutions rushed to include inerrancy in their doctrinal statements, whether they understood precisely what it meant or not. Even Carl Henry disagreed with Lindsell about the status of inerrancy as an essential of evangelical faith; he considered it essential to *consistent* evangelical thought, but he did not agree that one must affirm it in order to be an evangelical. Between 1977 and the new millennium, controversy over inerrancy consumed evangelical attention and energies. Numerous high-level conferences were held to attempt to define the concept and bring about some degree of reconciliation among evangelical parties that disagreed about it. The flagship evangelical seminary, Fuller Theological Seminary, resisted any attempt to force it to put inerrancy into its statement of faith. The National Association of Evangelicals retained "infallible" rather than "inerrant" as its description of Scripture's trustworthiness. On the other hand, many evangelical denominations and institutions began to use inerrancy as a litmus test for inclusion and acceptance.

Few evangelical theologians are willing to say that Scripture errs, but many say that "inerrant" is a misleading term for Scripture in that it implies the imposition of an alien standard of accuracy on an ancient text and detracts from the humanity and historicity of Scripture. In other words, it simply is not consistent with the actual phenomena of the biblical text. For them, "infallibility" is a stronger term than "inerrancy," in that a phone book can be inerrant without being infallible. Scripture's purpose is to identify God and communicate God's will as well as God's mercy and grace to humanity. So long as it does that successfully, whether it is "without error in the original autographs" is irrelevant.

A fourth area of tension within evangelical theology revolves around the rather amorphous issue of "evangelical boundaries." That is, which Christians and theological ideas are legitimately evangelical and which, though they may claim to be evangelical, are not? This has also to do with evangelical uses of nonevangelical thought and with evangelical dialogue with nonevangelicals, including Roman Catholics, Latter-day Saints (Mormons), liberal Protestants (including process theologians), and proponents of modernism (culture shaped by the Enlightenment) and postmodernism (culture in reaction to modernism but still rooted in the Enlightenment). Postfundamentalist evangelical founders and early leaders were never sure about Evangelicalism's precise limits and boundaries. According to their separatistic fundamentalist critics such as Carl McIntire, they demonstrated a lack of discernment about this matter when they admitted Pentecostals into the National Association of Evangelicals. On the other hand, they excluded any and all denominations and organizations that held membership in the mainline, more liberal Federal Council of Churches (later known as the National Council of Churches). Throughout its first almost fifty years of existence the National Association of Evangelicals has rejected such dual membership, while including within its ranks groups that fundamentalists (and perhaps some conservative evangelicals) consider heterodox. When the Evangelical Theological Society was founded, it required affirmation of biblical inerrancy for membership and has retained that, while adding belief in the Trinity (perhaps to exclude non-Trinitarian Pentecostals). Most, if not all, of the evangelical coalition's leaders wanted to expand evangelical boundaries to include both Reformed and Arminian perspectives on God's sovereignty and salvation, while keeping Reformed theology at the center of the coalition calling most of the shots.

Gradually two distinct viewpoints on evangelical identity developed within the evangelical coalition. For lack of better terminology we will here refer to them as the "broad view" and the "narrow view." No value judgment is intended with this terminology. All evangelicals agree that if Evangelicalism is compatible with anything and everything—even within Christendom—it is a meaningless concept, and its hopes for being an agent of renewal are dashed. The narrow-view evangelical theologians and leaders wish to identify and hold firm boundaries around Evangelicalism in order to stave off the seemingly inevitable "drift" toward doctrinal compromise and pluralism that has (at least according to conservative evangelicals) undermined the Christian witness of all mainline Protestant denominations and most of their churches and institutions. The broad-view evangelical theologians and leaders wish to expand Evangelicalism to include as many God-fearing, Jesus-loving, Bible-believing Christians as possible, while maintaining evangelical identity through a strong center of the movement. Narrow-view evangelicals fear that broad-view evangelicals will sell the soul of the movement through too much inclusion; broad-view evangelicals fear that narrow-view evangelicals will return the movement to fundamentalism. Of course, many evangelicals would not identify with either of these parties, but there are vocal leaders and thinkers within Evangelicalism who betray their sympathies by their responses to evangelical dialogue with nonevangelicals or to evangelical resolutions critical of greater diversity and inclusion within the movement.

The troubling issue of evangelical boundaries came up once again in the first year of the new millennium. The Evangelical Theological Society devoted its 2001 annual meeting to discussion about the matter and focused in particular on the open theism of Pinnock and others. Because several members of the ETS espoused that view of God and the future, it had become a matter of controversy within the ETS and the wider evangelical community. Several Reformed evangelical critics of open theism sought to exclude it and its proponents from Evangelicalism and the ETS by means of a resolution. The resolution that was passed by a majority of voting members of the society at its meeting in Colorado Springs in November 2001, however, stated only that God's knowledge of all events past, present, and future is certain and infallible. Much to the chagrin of some of the society's more conservative and fundamentalist members, open theists—including Pinnock—were not forced out. Whether their memberships will be dropped in the future, however, is uncertain.

Another boundary issue that creates tension within the evangelical theological community is related to evangelical appropriation of postmodern thought. This issue has been lurking in the background of evangelical discussion about boundaries throughout the 1990s and into the first decade of the new millennium, but it began to come to the foreground in 2001 at the ETS's annual meeting, devoted to evangelical boundaries. Controversy over evangelical uses of postmodern philosophy began with the 1995 publication of *Truth Is Stranger Than It Used to Be* (Downers Grove, IL: InterVarsity Press) by Canadian evangelical thinkers J. Richard Middleton and Brian J. Walsh. The authors claimed that postmodern philosophy's suspicion of all metanarratives (comprehensive worldviews) is compatible with the Bible's condemnations of idolatry and oppression. While affirming that the biblical narrative provides the one true metanarrative, Middleton and Walsh rejected any and all "totalizing metanarratives" on biblical grounds and argued that the Christian metanarrative is a liberating, antitotalizing one. Some evangelical critics felt they gave too much ground from under objective truth and accommodated too much to the relativistic spirit of the postmodern age. Sympathetic readers, however, discovered in *Truth Is Stranger Than It Used to Be* a refreshing departure from the conventional evangelical attacks on culture that are so often dependent on modern, Enlightenment modes of thinking.

The evangelical theologian who did more than anyone else to engage postmodernity from an evangelical perspective was Stanley J. Grenz. In a series of lectures, papers, and books Grenz presented a creative proposal for a postmodern evangelical theology that emphasizes the eschatological nature of truth and reality (drawing on the theology of Grenz's German mentor Wolfhart Pannenberg), the communal nature of Christianity (as opposed to modern individualism), and the narrative shape of revelation and the gospel message (using postliberal theologians such as Stanley Hauerwas). Grenz's systematic theology, *Theology for the Community of God* (Grand Rapids: Wm. B. Eerdmans, 2000), used the organizing theme of community to unite the various doctrinal loci and relegated the doctrine of Scripture to a section of the doctrine of the Holy Spirit. Like Middleton and Walsh and a variety of other postconservative evangelical thinkers who find an ally in some aspects of postmodernity, Grenz rejected Enlightenment foundationalist epistemology that seeks indubitable grounds for certainty outside of God's self-revelation in Jesus Christ and the narrative that identifies and makes him present to the believing community. Instead of viewing evangelical Christianity's essence as timeless truths in the form of revealed doctrines, he regarded it as the experience of "conversional piety" that takes place within the believing Christian community shaped by the gospel story. As in the case of Middleton and Walsh, critics of Grenz's project objected that it undermines the public, universal, propositional, and rational truth of the evangelical witness and ultimately succumbs to cultural relativism. Grenz and his defenders respond that such a critique is entirely based on outmoded Enlightenment (i.e., modernist) assumptions about the nature of truth and knowledge.

Some critics of evangelical engagement with postmodernity view the matter as a boundary issue and would like to restrict the evangelical community to those who reject postmodernism entirely. These narrow-view evangelicals are suspicious of evangelical appropriations of postmodern thought—however critical they may be—as dangerous, because they consider postmodernity irreducibly relativistic and worry that if the camel's nose of postmodernity is allowed under the evangelical tent, it will soon fill the whole tent and push out the objective truth of the gospel. Grenz and other broad-view evangelicals consider this concern overblown. Evangelicals have always appropriated elements of nonevangelical and even non-Christian philosophies—sometimes unwittingly. Conservative evangelicals such as Carl Henry and his followers used forms of foundationalism provided by Enlightenment thinkers such as Descartes and Locke and were heavily influenced by Scottish common sense realism—a British philosophy that responded to Hume's skepticism on the basis of a certain Enlightenment perspective. There is a great deal of interest in postmodernity among the younger evangelical students, pastors, and budding theologians. This greatly concerns many of the older evangelical thinkers who came to identify evangelical theology with the rational presuppositionalism and Reformed propositionalism of the leading evangelical thinkers of the 1950s. Some of them are mounting a concerted effort to enforce their narrow-view version of evangelical identity by portraying all postmodernity as negative deconstructionism that reduces to a relativistic ontology and pragmatic epistemology.

In spite of these points of tension within it and in spite of its diversity, evangelical theology has great vitality and significant unity. During the 1990s and into the first decade of the new millennium it has begun to emerge as a widely accepted legitimate theological alternative to mainline Protestant liberalism (e.g., process theology), liberationist theologies (e.g., radical feminism and Marxist-inspired Latin American liberation theology), and neo-orthodoxy (e.g., postliberal, Yale-New Haven theology). The future vitality and influence of evangelical theology will no doubt depend a great deal on harmony among evangelical theologians and the administrators who generally employ them in evangelical institutions. The greatest challenge facing them is striking the balance between unity and diversity within the evangelical theological community. Another challenge is retaining their basically conservative doctrinal identity while allowing and even affirming theological creativity within their ranks. At the moment most of the creative theological reflection and construction being done by evangelical theologians is taking place—and for the foreseeable future will be taking place—outside the power centers of conservative, establishment evangelical theological life (e.g., the Evangelical Theological Society and primary evangelical colleges and seminaries).

It seems that in order to break new ground in evangelical theology and think in fresh and imaginative ways, evangelical theologians must be free of the hindrances of ecclesiastical political conservatism and the fundamentalist habits of the mind that still regulate much of evangelical administration. Leading the way into Evangelicalism's theological reform are such young, innovate thinkers as Miroslav Volf, Stanley J. Grenz, Kevin Vanhoozer, Nancey Murphy, and John Sanders. Leading the way in maintaining the status quo of the "received evangelical tradition" and guarding Evangelicalism's traditional theological identity and boundaries are Millard Erickson, Wayne Grudem, Norman Geisler, and Al Mohler Jr. It would be to evangelical theology's great detriment if these thinkers and their followers ceased having dialogue with one another so that evangelical theology broke into two camps ignoring each other or even casting uninformed aspersions at one another. The future of evangelical theology depends on harmony, if not agreement, between these two groups of influential evangelical thinkers.

An index for this volume may be found online by clicking a link on the IVP webpage for *Pocket History of Evangelical Theology* at:

www.ivpress.com/cgi-ivpress/book.pl/code=2706